Understanding key legal issues

The role of ASIC

Disclaimer

Wolters Kluwer

Understanding key legal issues

The role of ASIC

2022

CCH AUSTRALIA LIMITED
GPO Box 4072, Sydney, NSW 2001
Head Office Macquarie Park
Phone: (02) 9857 1300 Fax: (02) 9857 1600
Customer Support
Phone: 1 300 300 224 Fax: 1 300 306 224
https://shop.wolterskluwer.com.au
Book Code: 10097746-0001

ABOUT WOLTERS KLUWER

Wolters Kluwer is a leading provider of accurate, authoritative and timely information services for professionals across the globe. We create value by combining information, deep expertise and technology to provide our customers with solutions that improve their quality and effectiveness. Professionals turn to us when they need actionable information to better serve their clients.

With the integrity and accuracy of over 45 years' experience in Australia and New Zealand, and over 175 years internationally, Wolters Kluwer is lifting the standard in software, knowledge, tools and education.

Wolters Kluwer — When you have to be right.

Enquiries are welcome on **1 300 300 224**.

"Cataloguing-in-Publication Data available through the National Library of Australia."

First edition 2022

ISBN 978-1-922847-02-7

TABLE OF CONTENTS

Page

Page

FOREWORD

The Australian Securities and Investments Commission (ASIC) has been a cornerstone of corporate regulation since its inception, in its current form, in 1998. It permeates all aspects of corporate, securities and financial services, including consumer protection in superannuation, insurance, deposit-taking and credit.

ASIC is the primary body responsible for carrying out the administrative functions as set out in the Corporations Act, and ASIC's role and operations fall within the ministerial responsibility of the Commonwealth Treasurer.

A significant part of ASIC's resources are dedicated to the regulation of financial markets and consumer protection functions in relation to the financial system generally. Any party involved in running a business should be aware of ASIC's role, responsibilities, obligations and duties. This is essential both to ensure compliance with company law but also to seek the support of ASIC where required. A large part of ASIC's role is to assist with the setting up and running of a company. This role includes:

Registering companies

ASIC maintains a Register of Companies for the purpose of registering new corporations in order to allow them to become incorporated, and changing the details of existing corporations.

Gathering and disseminating information about companies

Companies are required to provide ASIC with certain information about their participants, their operations and their financial affairs. ASIC maintains a record of that information and makes that information available – via a company search – to any party who may be interested in the affairs of the company.

Educating companies and individuals about the law

ASIC issues Regulatory Guides, Information Sheets and other publications which are designed to assist parties in understanding, and complying with, the Corporations Act and other legislation which governs the operations of businesses.

Modifying the Corporations Act in certain circumstances

ASIC has the power to modify the operation of, or grant exemptions from, certain provisions of the Corporations Act in certain situations. In this way, the law can be adjusted to take account of special circumstances without the need to include special arrangements in the Corporations Act to deal with every possible contingency or unusual circumstance, however remote or unlikely.

Registering company auditors and liquidators

ASIC is responsible for registering parties who are qualified to act as corporate auditors or liquidators.

Investigating breaches of the law and taking enforcement action

ASIC has both formal and informal powers in order to investigate suspected breaches of the Corporations Act. These investigations may occur as the result of a party raising a complaint directly with ASIC. Following an investigation, ASIC can enforce the law, if need be, by taking certain administrative action. This may include revoking a licence or issuing a banning order to, for example, ban an individual from managing a corporation for a set period of time. ASIC can bring an action for breach of the civil penalty provisions under Pt 9.4B of the Corporations Act, bring civil proceedings under s 50 of the ASIC Act on behalf of parties harmed by breaches of the Corporations Act or refer a breach to the Commonwealth Director of Public Prosecutions for criminal prosecution.

In performing its role, and exercising its powers, ASIC is required by legislation to meet the objectives as set out in s 1(2) of the *Australian Securities and Investments Commission Act 2001 (Cth)*, including:

- maintaining, facilitating and improving the performance of the financial system and the companies, and other entities, within that system, in the interests of commercial certainty in the marketplace, reducing business costs and the efficiency and development of the economy, and
- promoting the confident and informed participation of investors and consumers in the financial system.

Although ASIC has come under scrutiny for a somewhat lenient approach to regulation, particularly following the Banking Royal Commission, there is little doubt when it comes to ASIC's effectiveness in taking enforcement action as a litigator. Indeed, in the 10 years between 2010 and 2020, ASIC have been successful, or partly successful, in 88% of civil litigation enforcement actions undertaken in the Federal Court (including the full court) and the High Court.

As we move into a new post-Covid era in 2022 and beyond, together with a new hybrid way of working and communicating, we will continue to see ASIC's role expanding to embrace the new corporate landscape. ASIC's corporate plan for 2022–26, which was released on 22 August 2022, outlines its strategic objectives for the next 4 years. This includes such responsibilities as:

- **Product design and distribution** — Reduce the risk of harm to consumers of financial and credit products, caused by poor product design, distribution and marketing, by driving compliance with the new design and distribution obligations.
- **Sustainable finance** — Support market integrity through proactive supervision and enforcement of governance, transparency and disclosure standards in relation to sustainable finance.
- **Retirement decision making** — Protect consumers, particularly as they plan and make decisions for retirement, with a focus on superannuation products, managed investments and financial advice.
- **Technology risks** — Focus on the impacts of technology in financial markets and services i.e. the emergence of FinTech, drive good cyber-risk and operational resilience practices and act to address digitally-enabled misconduct, including scams.

These responsibilities address a number of emerging trends and important law reforms which are reshaping Australia's financial system, including digitally enabled misconduct, emerging technologies, climate risks for corporations and Australia's ageing population.

Now, more than ever, it is important for any party involved in business to be aware of, and understand, the key role of our corporate regulator. This concise summary of ASIC's role can assist you in understanding what you need to know.

Wolters Kluwer ©

1 September 2022

PREFACE

This brand new publication has been compiled in order to provide readers with a **concise summary** of the role of one of Australia's most important regulators within the corporate space — the Australian Securities and Investments Commission (ASIC).

We hear a lot about ASIC in the day-to-day news — be that:

- introducing new policy or regulations
- tightening regulation of financial providers following the Royal Commission into Misconduct in the Banking, Superannuation and Financial Services Industry (Banking Royal Commission), or
- holding corporations, and those behind a corporation such as individual directors, to account, often via litigation in the courts.

ASIC was originally formed as the Australian Securities Commission, established on 1 January 1991 by the (then) *Australian Securities Commission Act 1989 (Cth).* The role of the Australian Securities Commission was to unify corporate regulators around Australia by replacing the National Companies and Securities Commission and the Corporate Affairs offices of the States and Territories.

The corporate regulator became what we now know as ASIC on 1 July 1998, when it also became responsible for consumer protection in superannuation, insurance and deposit taking. Since that date ASIC has gained further responsibilities, namely for credit in 2002, for the Australian Stock Exchange in 2009 and for the Chi-X in 2011. ASIC's role continues to expand to increased scrutiny of financial service providers, following the scathing report handed down by the Banking Royal Commission in February 2019.

Hence it appears that ASIC is infiltrating more of the corporate market, with increased responsibilities — often justifiably so. **But do we really fully understand the role, responsibilities, duties and obligations of ASIC?**

ASIC's role is to regulate company and financial services and enforce laws in order to protect Australian investors, creditors and consumers. It does this via its administrative responsibility over several legislative Acts and its reporting to government. ASIC exists as an independent commission of the Australian government and reports directly to the Treasurer. It is this independence, autonomy and impartiality which is the cornerstone for ensuring that the Australian public — and in particular those dealing with corporations, as investors, financiers, creditors or consumers — are adequately protected.

Hence, the role of our corporate regulator is necessarily broad in order to regulate, monitor and enforce compliance with Australia's corporate and financial legislation — being primarily the *Corporations Act 2001 (Cth)* and the *Australian Securities and Investments Commission Act 2001 (Cth)* from which ASIC derives its powers.

ASIC's role includes responsibility for:

- corporate governance
- financial services
- securities and derivatives
- insurance
- consumer protection, and
- financial literacy.

ASIC's role has come under increased scrutiny over the last few years, particularly in the wake of the Banking Royal Commission. The Banking Royal Commission uncovered some abhorrent behaviour within the banking and financial services industry including charging excessive fees, failing to fully disclose significant information in relation to financial products, financial advice or fees, promoting financial products unsuitable for the particular individual in question and taking advantage of those most vulnerable within the system. A significant amount of this behaviour lay with the big 4 banks. However, smaller and independent financial providers were also at fault. ASIC came under increased criticism by consumers, consumer advocates and public officials over what was perceived as inaction and inefficiencies in protecting consumers, particularly those more vulnerable, from the actions of large financial institutions. Indeed, going back as far as 2016, ASIC was subject to heavy criticism in the initial debate concerning the creation of a Royal Commission into banking and financial services — no doubt due, at least in part, to the scrutiny to which ASIC, and its operations, would be subjected to as a result.

The aim of this publication is to provide you with an introductory snapshot of ASIC's current role, responsibilities and obligations. It is not intended to be a complete all-encompassing expose of ASIC's duties. Rather it focuses on the principal roles of ASIC as a regulator and a litigator within the corporate and financial sector. There is a specific focus on ASIC's role in regulating unconscionable conduct within the financial services sector and protecting consumers. This is even more important following the Banking Royal Commission's report and, as a result, ASIC has been provided with enhanced powers to ensure that financial service providers are subjected to the level of scrutiny as recommended by the Commission.

Further information on any of the topics presented in this publication can be obtained from our comprehensive company law commentary on our award-winning Pinpoint ® platform. This commentary contains a chapter dedicated to ASIC in order to assist you in understanding the role of our corporate regulator in more detail, including in-depth case analysis with a focus on ASIC as a litigator.

ASIC's website – at asic.gov.au – also provides a wealth of information on the role of our corporate regulator, as well as supplementary material for corporations, directors, investors, creditors, financiers, small businesses and individuals. This includes regulatory instruments which provide ASIC with the powers to carry out its role and responsibilities, media releases, ASIC's corporate plan and the ability to search ASIC's business registers.

Hence, our company law commentary, and the information available direct from ASIC, is designed to supplement and build on the information presented in this publication. Understanding the role of our corporate regulator is essential for any business to survive and thrive in an increasingly complex corporate environment.

Wolters Kluwer ©

1 September 2022

WOLTERS KLUWER ACKNOWLEDGMENTS

Wolters Kluwer wishes to thank the following persons who contributed to, and supported, this publication:

Director, General Manager, Research & Learning, Wolters Kluwer Asia Pacific:

Lauren Ma

Associate Director, Regional Head of Content, Wolters Kluwer Asia Pacific:

Diana Winfield

Head of Legal Content, Wolters Kluwer Australia:

Carol Louw

Barrister-at-law, Legal Content Editor (Company Law):

Nicholas Bentley

UTS Faculty of Law Lecturer:

Dr Robin Bowley

Lawyer, Legal Content Editor (Company Law):

June Ahern

Chapter 1

INTRODUCTION TO THE AUSTRALIAN SECURITIES AND INVESTMENTS COMMISSION (ASIC)

¶1-000 Overview

The Australian Securities and Investments Commission (ASIC) is, put simply, Australia's **corporate regulator**. It is an independent Australian government body. Its role is to ensure that corporations and financial institutions comply with their statutory obligations under various Commonwealth, State and Territory legislation, as well as taking enforcement action for non-compliance, which may involve a process of investigation and information-gathering. Hence, ASIC has a role as both a regulator and a litigator.

Responsibility for the day-to-day administration of the *Corporations Act 2001 (Cth)* (Corporations Act), which governs Australia's corporate bodies, is vested largely in ASIC, as well as a number of ancillary bodies. ASIC's functions and powers are provided for in the *Australian Securities and Investments Commission Act 2001 (Cth)* (ASIC Act).

There is now a single national scheme for the regulation of Australian corporations. The ASIC Act, together with the Corporations Act, was created as a result of the States and Territories referring their relevant legislative powers in relation to the formation of corporations, corporate regulation and the regulation of financial services & products to the Commonwealth in accordance with s 51(xxxvii) of the Constitution. This created a role for ASIC, as our Federal corporate regulator.

¶1-010 The ASIC Act

The 2001 ASIC Act essentially re-enacted the 1989 ASIC Act, as a Commonwealth Act capable of national operation, in contrast to the previous aggregation of State, Territory and Federal laws. As a result of that re-enactment, the following bodies, established under the 1989 ASIC legislation continue to exist. The:

- Australian Securities and Investments Commission (ASIC itself)
- Companies Auditors Disciplinary Board — formerly known as the Companies Auditors and Liquidators Disciplinary Board (CALDB)
- Takeovers Panel
- Financial Reporting Council (FRC)
- Australian Accounting Standards Board (AASB) and the Office of the Australian Accounting Standards Board
- Auditing & Assurance Standards Board (AUASB) and the Office of the Auditing & Assurance Standards Board, and
- Parliamentary Joint Committee on Corporations and Financial Services.

The ASIC Act imposes obligations upon these bodies, relating to their financing, staffing and reporting duties. Part 4, Div 2 of the ASIC Act (ss 97 – 101) permits the setting up of separate divisions of ASIC, where each division is essentially treated as an independent Commission. This includes the Takeovers Panel and the Companies Auditors Disciplinary Board.

Section 4 of the ASIC Act provides that the Act applies in "this jurisdiction". This term is defined in s 5 of the Corporations Act as the referring States and Territories. It can also apply to States which are not referring States, to the extent that the application would be within the Commonwealth's legislative powers. Part 2, Div 2 of the ASIC Act (relating to unconscionable conduct and consumer protection in financial services, ss 12AC – 12HD) is intended to operate concurrently with common law remedies and remedies available under other statutes, except where a contrary indication is expressed.

To the extent that the ASIC Act does not provide to the contrary, Pt 1.2 of the Corporations Act (which contains the interpretation provisions) has an equivalent application to the ASIC Act, ss 5(2) and (3) of the ASIC Act. Hence, for clarification, an expression in the ASIC Act can have the same meaning as in the Corporations Act.

ASIC has published various documents which explain its role and how it carries out that role. These documents are available on ASIC's website, at asic.gov.au. They include:

- *ASIC Service Charter* — This sets out what a party can expect when they deal with ASIC, and how a party can help ASIC to serve them better. It explains how ASIC responds to requests (for example, when applying for licences or relief from the law) and how ASIC responds when a party reports alleged misconduct by corporations or individuals.
- *What we do* — This document sets out ASIC's role and its approach to this role. It also documents how ASIC is organised, consults, and is held accountable.

¶1-020 ASIC's Objectives

Section 1 of the ASIC Act sets out the objects of the Act. Section 1(2) requires ASIC, when performing its role and exercising its powers, to strive to:

(a) maintain, facilitate and improve the performance of the financial system and the entities within that system in the interests of commercial certainty, reducing business costs, and the efficiency and development of the economy

(b) promote the confident and informed participation of investors and consumers in the financial system

(d) administer the laws which confer functions and powers on it effectively and with a minimum of procedural requirements

(e) receive, process and store, efficiently and quickly, the information provided to ASIC under the laws which confer functions and powers on it

(f) ensure that information is available as soon as practicable for access by the public, and

(g) take whatever action it can take, and is necessary, in order to enforce and give effect to the laws of the Commonwealth which confer functions and powers on it.

Section 1(2A) requires ASIC to "consider the effects that the performance of its functions and the exercise of its powers will have on competition in the financial system". This amendment was brought about by the *Treasury Laws Amendment (Enhancing ASIC's Capabilities) Act 2018 (Cth)*. The Explanatory Memorandum (EM) to the Treasury Laws Amendment (Enhancing ASIC's Capabilities) Bill 2018 noted that an explicit reference to take competition issues into account obliges ASIC to consciously consider how its actions may impact on competition in the financial system. Hence, this enables ASIC to favour one option over another due to its effects on competition. The EM advises ASIC that some of the specific aspects of competition to which ASIC may have regard include whether:

- a decision will create a barrier to entry for new firms to enter the industry
- a decision will create regulatory advantages for some corporations over others competing in the same market sector, or generally across the industry as a whole
- a decision will allow consumers to exert demand-side competitive pressure in a marketplace
- a decision will disproportionately impact small corporate entities (for example by imposing obligations which do not appropriately match the regulatory risks as presented by those entities) and the impact which that could have on competition
- alternative competitively-neutral approaches can be identified.

The EM also states that competition should not be considered in isolation; rather, ASIC should consider competition in conjunction with the elements as listed in s 1(2) of the ASIC Act, such as striving to improve the performance of the financial system and promoting commercial certainty, investment opportunities, economic development and efficiency whilst reducing business costs. For example, ASIC may decide to proceed with an intervention which has a detrimental impact on competition because the intervention would significantly improve confident and informed participation by investors in the market. Hence, ASIC is required to determine the appropriate weight it will give to competition, as compared to increased investment, based on the relevant circumstances.

In cases where competition is not relevant to how ASIC performs its role and exercises its powers (for example, internal corporate functions), ASIC can note that competition has no bearing on the function or power.

The roles and powers of ASIC are also detailed in s 11 of the ASIC Act as outlined below.

¶1-030 ASIC's Legislative Functions and Other Roles

Section 11 of the ASIC Act outlines ASIC's role under both the ASIC Act and the Corporations Act, other than the excluded provisions (s 12A and Pt 2, Div 2 of the ASIC Act, which relate to unconscionable conduct and consumer protection in financial services, ss 12AC – 12HD).

As you will see throughout this publication, both the ASIC Act and the Corporations Act confer specific legislative powers on ASIC to carry out roles such as investigations, information-gathering and hearings, for the purposes of ensuring corporate compliance with the relevant legislation, s 11(1) of the ASIC Act.

Under s 11 of the ASIC Act, ASIC also has the following roles:

ASIC's role in providing support

Sections 11(2)(a) and (aa) of the ASIC Act, oblige ASIC to provide such staff and support to the Takeovers Panel, the Companies Auditors Disciplinary Board and Financial Services and Credit Panels, as are required to permit those bodies to perform their functions and exercise their powers.

ASIC's role in legislative advice and law reform

Section 11(2)(b) of the ASIC Act requires ASIC to inform the Minister of any changes to the ASIC Act or Corporations Act, which ASIC believes are necessary in order to allow ASIC to perform its duties. This legislative advice does not extend to the excluded provisions (s 12A and Pt 2, Div 2 of the ASIC Act, relating to unconscionable conduct and consumer protection in financial services, ss 12AC – 12HD).

Section 11(3) of the ASIC Act permits ASIC to advise the Minister, and make any recommendations as it sees fit, regarding:

- companies, or a segment of the financial services industry, including proposals to improve the efficiency of financial markets, ss 11(3)(d) and (e)
- a proposal to draft new provisions, or amend existing provisions, in a process of law reform, of the ASIC Act or the Corporations Act, ss 11(3)(a) and (c) of the ASIC Act
- the operation or administration, in practice, of the ASIC Act or the Corporations Act, s 11(3)(b).

Note that any reference to the ASIC Act in s11(3) does not extend to the excluded provisions.

Section 11(4) of the ASIC Act confers a broad power on ASIC to do whatever is necessary for, or in connection with, or reasonably incidental to the performance of its roles. This confers a wide discretionary power on ASIC, beyond just that as mandated by the legislation.

Section 11(6) of the ASIC Act confirms that ASIC has general administration of the Act.

ASIC's role in acting as agent for a State or Territory

Section 11(8) of the ASIC Act permits ASIC, with the consent of the Minister, to enter into an agreement with a State or Territory to allow ASIC to exercise its powers and perform its role, as an agent of the State or Territory. As a result, ASIC will have such functions and powers as are conveyed by such an agreement; however, ASIC is still not obliged to actually perform such functions or exercise such powers, s 11(9) of the ASIC Act. Again, this conveys a very broad power on ASIC.

Under s 11(9A) of the ASIC Act, ASIC may have roles or powers conferred by a State or Territory law if:

- that law provides for the amendment, repeal or termination of any of the repealed legislation under the *Financial Sector Reform (Amendments and Transitional Provisions) Act (No.1) 1999 (Cth)*, Sch 8, Item 22, and
- the conferral of the powers or roles are in accordance with an agreement between the Commonwealth and the State or Territory in question, or an approval provided by the Minister.

However, like s 11(9), ASIC is not obliged to perform such roles, or exercise such powers.

ASIC's role in audit performance and compliance

Section 11(10) of the ASIC Act permits ASIC, with ministerial consent, to enter into an agreement or arrangement with a regulatory body of a foreign country under which ASIC undertakes to assist that regulatory body to ascertain whether Australian auditors comply with audit requirements which are imposed by, or under, laws of that foreign country, or adopted as professional standards in that foreign country. Ministerial consent, under s 11(10) of the ASIC Act, may be revoked by the Minister in writing, s 11(11) of the ASIC Act. If ASIC *does* enter into an agreement under s 11(10) of the ASIC Act, ASIC must as soon as practicable, publish a notice in the *Gazette* setting out the particulars of the regulatory body in question, the particulars of the agreement and the audit requirements to which the agreement relates, s 11(12) of the ASIC Act. A notice published in the Gazette is not a legislative instrument, s 11(13) of the ASIC Act.

When it comes to audit compliance, ASIC is entrusted with the following roles under the ASIC Act:

Section 11(14)(a) of the ASIC Act permits ASIC to assist a regulatory body, with which ASIC has entered an agreement under s 11(10), in examining the policies and working practices of an Australian auditor, so as to assist the regulatory body in determining compliance with the audit requirements as stipulated in the agreement. In performing this role, ASIC may examine policies and working practices of an auditor in general, or in their application to specific audits, s 11(15) of the ASIC Act.

Section 11(14)(b) of the ASIC Act allows ASIC to disclose to a regulatory body, with which ASIC has entered an agreement under s 11(10) of the ASIC Act, the information obtained by ASIC in assisting in such an examination.

However, pursuant to s 11(16) of the ASIC Act, ASIC is again under no obligation to perform a role or exercise a power under s 11(14) of the ASIC Act.

ASIC's role as regulator of a passport fund

Section 11(16A) of the ASIC Act confers on ASIC the roles and powers of a home or host regulator for a passport fund. However, again ASIC is under no duty or obligation to perform such a role or exercise such powers.

What is a passport fund?

A passport fund is essentially an investment vehicle which offers interest in funds. An entity is an eligible passport fund if it is both:

- a collective investment scheme (CIS) which is regulated by the corporations legislation of a participating economy. In Australia, the corporations legislation comprises the ASIC Act and the Corporations Act, and
- the CIS is registered as a passport fund in a participating economy, such as Australia.

To become a passport fund, eligible funds and operators, must apply to the home economy regulator for registration as a passport fund. Once approved, the fund must then apply to the host economy for approval to enter and offer fund interests in the host jurisdiction. Hence, s 11(16A) permits ASIC to exercise the powers and functions of both a home economy regulator and a host economy in Australia.

ASIC's roles and ministerial direction

Section 11(17) of the ASIC Act confirms that ASIC is not subject to any ministerial direction in relation to:

- Entering into an agreement under s 11(8) of the ASIC Act, which permits ASIC to act as agent of a State or Territory
- Performing a role, or exercising a power, referred to in s 11(9) of the ASIC Act, which allows ASIC to decide whether to act as agent of a State or Territory, or
- Performing a role under ss 11(9A) or 11(14), which relates to audit compliance, or 11(16A), which relates to regulation of a passport fund.

¶1-040 ASIC's General Administration, Role and Powers

Under s 11 of the ASIC Act, ASIC has general administration of the Act, and has such functions and powers as are conferred on it by, or under, the Corporations Act, other than the excluded provisions (s 12A and Pt 2, Div 2 of the ASIC Act, relating to unconscionable conduct and consumer protection in financial services, ss 12AC – 12HD). There is also scope under s 11 for ASIC, with the Minister's consent, to enter into agreements or arrangements with a State or Territory as an agent of that State or Territory.

Monitoring audit compliance

ASIC may also, with ministerial consent, enter into an agreement or arrangement with a regulatory body of a foreign country under which ASIC undertakes to assist that regulatory body to ascertain whether Australian auditors comply with **audit requirements** which are imposed by, or under, laws of that foreign country, or adopted as professional standards in that foreign country: ss 11(10) – (17). Although these provisions are not specific to any particular foreign country, the EM to the Australian Securities and Investments Commission Amendment (Audit Inspection) Bill 2006 made it clear that they are intended to enable ASIC to enter into a mutual cooperative arrangement with the United States Public Company Accounting Oversight Board (PCAOB). The single, joint inspection arrangement proposed under the cooperative arrangement between ASIC and the PCAOB reduces the regulatory burden and eliminates duplicated processes relating to audit inspections.

Regulating unconscionable conduct and protecting consumers

Part 2, Div 2 of the ASIC Act contains extensive provisions (ss 12AC – 12HD) regulating unconscionable conduct and consumer protection in the provision of financial services. Refer to Chapter 6 for further details. This regime closely mirrors the provisions of the *Competition and Consumer Act 2010 (Cth)* and supports ASIC's role in relation to the enforcement of Chapter 7 of the Corporations Act (relating to financial services & markets).

Carrying out investigations

Under Pt 3, Div 1 of the ASIC Act (ss 13 – 18), ASIC has the power to carry out investigations, where it has reason to suspect that a contravention of one, or more, of a number of laws has been committed. Where ASIC is carrying out an investigation it may examine certain persons under oath, Pt 3, Div 2 (ss 19 – 27). Hence, an examination may form part of an investigation, although this will depend largely on the circumstances and may not be required in each case. Certain consequences arising out of an examination, such as how the examination is to be conducted, who can be present at an examination, and who can obtain copies of the examination transcript, are also covered by this Division.

Inspecting books and gathering information

Under Pt 3, Div 3 of the ASIC Act (ss 28 – 39C), ASIC may inspect books, either in general or for the purposes of a specific investigation, for ASIC to ensure that it can carry out its role.

ASIC can require certain parties, such as those in the financial services industry (financial advisers and brokers, amongst others) to disclose information under Pt 3, Div 4 of the ASIC Act (ss 40 – 48). Disclosure obligations can also be imposed on certain officers of a corporation, in relation to financial products.

Proceedings and hearings

Following an investigation or examination, ASIC may bring proceedings under Pt 3, Div 5 of the ASIC Act (ss 49 and 50).

Part 3, Div 6 of the ASIC Act (ss 51 – 62) permits ASIC to hold its own hearings in certain circumstances. Other bodies administered by ASIC, such as the Takeovers Panel and the Companies Auditors Disciplinary Board can hold their own proceedings and hearings under Pt 10, Div 3 (ss 187 – 201A for the Takeovers Panel) and Pt 11, Div 2 (ss 215 – 223 for the Companies Auditors Disciplinary Board) respectively.

Prosecuting offences

Part 3, Div 7 of the ASIC Act (ss 63 – 70) lists offences against the Act. Offences which are partly committed in more than one jurisdiction can be deemed to be committed in one of those jurisdictions.

ASIC's power to deal with **non-compliance** against Pt 3 is contained in Pt 3, Div 8 of the ASIC Act (ss 71 – 75).

Part 3A of the ASIC Act (ss 93A – 93BA) focuses on enforceable undertakings (essentially a form of remedy) in relation to registered schemes, foreign passport funds and corporate collective investment vehicles (a new means of investment).

Admitting evidence

The admissibility and weight of evidence to be used in proceedings is dealt with in Pt 3, Div 9 of the ASIC Act. However, a reference to "proceedings" excludes those hearings before the Takeovers Panel or the Companies Auditors Disciplinary Board.

Miscellaneous functions

Part 3, Div 10 of the ASIC Act (ss 84 – 93AA) contains miscellaneous provisions for the purposes of ASIC investigations and information-gathering, which do not naturally fall within another part of the Act. This includes the following provisions:

- Section 86 – The service of documents
- Section 87 – Specifying a time and place for the production of books

- Section 88 – Application of the *Crimes Act 1914 (Cth)* (Crimes Act) and the *Evidence Act 1995 (Cth)* (Evidence Act), to provisions under the ASIC Act
- Sections 89, 90 and 91 – Handling expenses associated with an ASIC investigation
- Section 93AA – Enforcement of written undertakings (essentially a form of remedy) provided to ASIC.

Likewise, Pt 15 of the ASIC Act (ss 243B – 251) contains similar miscellaneous provisions for the operation of the Act as a whole. These provisions include:

- Section 243C – ASIC publication of information relating to internal dispute resolution
- Section 243D – Reporting suspicious cash transactions to ASIC
- Section 243E – Reporting suspected anti-money laundering or counter-terrorism financing to ASIC
- Section 244 – Review of ASIC decisions by the Administrative Appeals Tribunal

¶1-050 ASIC as a Body Corporate

ASIC is defined as a body corporate under s 8(1)(a) of the ASIC Act. However, under s 8(1A), and for the purposes of finance law – within the meaning of the *Public Governance, Performance and Accountability Act 2013 (Cth)* – ASIC is not recognised as a body corporate.

The fact that ASIC is a body corporate (other than for the purposes of finance law as described above) means that the decisions of its members (often referred to as "commissioners") when acting as ASIC cannot be made the subject of review under the *Administrative Decisions (Judicial Review) Act 1977 (Cth)*: *Somerville v ASC* (1993) 11 ACLC 1. In *Somerville's* case, it was also held that there was no cause of action under s 39B of the *Judiciary Act 1903 (Cth)* against the commissioners when they were acting as ASIC and the commission's actions were already subject to review under the Administrative Decisions (Judicial Review) Act.

Membership of ASIC

Under s 9 of the ASIC Act, ASIC must have at least 3 (and no more than 8) members, who are appointed by the Governor-General. ASIC must have a chairperson who is a full-time member of ASIC and is appointed by the Governor-General. Pursuant to s 10 of the ASIC Act, ASIC may have up to 2 deputy chairpersons, who are also full-time members, and are appointed by the Governor-General. Section 118 of the ASIC Act permits the Minister to appoint an ASIC member as acting deputy chairperson if there are fewer than 2 persons holding the office of deputy chairperson, or while a deputy chairperson is absent from office or is acting as chairperson: s 118.

ASIC Delegates

Under Pt 4, Div 3 (s 102) of the ASIC Act, ASIC can delegate its powers or functions to another party. Acts done by delegates are taken to have been done by ASIC under s 102(6). However, unlike commissioners, delegates may find their decisions subject to review under the *Administrative Decisions (Judicial Review) Act 1977 (Cth)*, or themselves subject to proceedings under s 39B of the *Judiciary Act 1903 (Cth)*: *Somerville & Ors v Australian Securities Commission & Ors* (1993) 11 ACLC 1.

Financial Accountability and ASIC

From 1 July 2014, the *Public Governance, Performance and Accountability Act 2013 (Cth)* is the primary financial legislation of the Commonwealth.

ASIC's status as a regulator means it needs to be able to take enforcement action against the Commonwealth itself and hence requires a separate legal identity. However, as a temporary measure, s 8(1A) of the ASIC Act treats ASIC as a non-corporate Commonwealth entity for the purposes of finance law. This ensures that ASIC has access to the appropriations provisions of the Public Governance, Performance and Accountability Act. For the purposes of finance law, ASIC is a listed entity. ASIC's chairperson is the accountable authority of ASIC, and the chairperson and other members of ASIC are officials under s 9A of the ASIC Act.

ASIC also has responsibility for the holding and handling of **unclaimed property**. For property, which is not money, ASIC must sell or dispose of the property as it sees fit. Unclaimed property, including funds and proceeds from the sale of property, is remitted directly to the Commonwealth Consolidated Revenue Fund upon receipt by ASIC.

Owners of unclaimed property can claim and receive the return of an amount equal to the value of their property, funded by an amount appropriated by Parliament for that purpose. They may also be entitled to the payment of interest under ss 1339 and 1341 of the Corporations Act.

Chapter 2
DIVISIONS OF ASIC

ASIC may set up several additional divisions in order to assist in performing its role and exercising its powers.

This chapter discusses how ASIC establishes its divisions to assist it in performing its functions and role, as well as providing an overview of a number of disciplinary bodies for which ASIC has an administrative role.

¶2-000 Creating Divisions of ASIC

The substantive provisions of the ASIC Act which relate to the creation of ASIC divisions are summarised below:

Establishing a division of ASIC

Under s 97 of the ASIC Act, ASIC may establish a division by a direction in writing. The newly established division must consist of at least 2 specified members to perform or exercise the specific role, functions and powers of ASIC, s 97(1). A chairperson must also be appointed, s 97(2).

Under s 98 of the ASIC Act, the effect of establishing a division is that a newly established ASIC division can perform all the functions and powers of ASIC, ss 98(1) and (2). Indeed, a meeting of a division of ASIC is deemed to be a meeting of ASIC, s 98(4).

Reconstituting a division of ASIC

Sections 99 and 100 of the ASIC Act permit ASIC to reconstitute a division of ASIC. This means that a direction to establish a division of ASIC, under s 97 of the ASIC Act, may be revoked or amended, in relation to membership, or in any other respect, s 99.

If there is an amendment to a division of ASIC so as to change that division's membership, pursuant to s 99, and that division had commenced, but not yet completed, the performance of some of its functions or powers, then the newly constituted division may complete the matter, s 100.

Multiple divisions of ASIC

Section 101 of the ASIC Act allows for the establishment of multiple divisions of ASIC. These divisions may perform the same functions or exercise the same powers simultaneously.

¶2-010 ASIC's Role in Relation to Other Disciplinary Bodies

The ASIC Act also provides ASIC with the power to convene other disciplinary bodies, each focused on different specific functions or target areas under the general umbrella of corporate governance.

Although, the focus of this publication remains a discussion and analysis of ASIC's core functions and role under the ASIC Act, these disciplinary bodies warrant mention and consideration. An overview of these bodies is provided below. More detailed information on these disciplinary bodies is beyond the scope of this publication but can be found by direct reference to the legislation and ASIC's guidance material.

The Financial Services and Credit Panel

Section 139 of the ASIC Act (Pt 9, Div 1) permits ASIC to convene a Financial Services and Credit Panel. Part 9 was added to the ASIC Act by the *Financial Sector Reform (Hayne Royal Commission Response – Better Advice) Act 2021 (Cth)*, which commenced on 1 January 2022, largely in response to repercussions from the Banking Royal Commission. The Financial Services and Credit Panel will exist within ASIC as a disciplinary body for financial advisers.

Part 9 of the ASIC Act (Divs 1 – 7, ss 139 – 171F) governs the formation and conduct of the Financial Services and Credit Panel, including:

- the appointment of panel members – Pt 9, Div 2, ss 140 – 147
- the decisions of panels, both at meetings and without meetings – Pt 9, Div 3, ss 148 – 156
- conducting a panel hearing, including the applicable offence provisions – Pt 9, Div 4, ss 157 – 171C
- disclosure of information to panel members – Pt 9, Div 5, s 171D
- enforceable undertakings (as a form of remedy) – Pt 9, Div 6, s 171E, and
- electronic communication of documents – Pt 9, Div 7, s 171F.

The Takeovers Panel

Part 10 of the ASIC Act (ss 172 – 201A) governs the conduct of Australia's Takeovers Panel. This panel was originally established under s 171 of the *Australian Securities Commission Act 1989 (Cth)*. When that Act was repealed and replaced by the current ASIC Act, the continued existence of the Takeovers Panel was empowered by s 261 of the Act. Section 261 allows for a body which was established under the old ASIC Act to continue in existence as if it has been established under the existing ASIC Act.

The Takeovers Panel is an Australian government peer review body which regulates corporate control transactions, primarily by the resolution of takeover disputes, during the takeover bid period. The Panel has the power to declare "unacceptable circumstances" in relation to a takeover, or proposed takeover, of an Australian corporation or listed managed investment scheme.

Unacceptable circumstances may arise, for example, where a proposed acquisition will unnecessarily hinder competition in the marketplace or lead to a monopoly.

Part 10 of the ASIC Act (Divs 1 – 3, ss 172 – 201A) governs the conduct of the Takeovers Panel, including:

- Membership of the Panel – Pt 10, Div 1, ss 172 – 183
- Conduct of the Panel's business – Pt 10, Div 2, ss 184 – 186
- Panel proceedings – Pt 10, Div 3, ss 187 – 201A.

The Companies Auditors Disciplinary Board

Part 11 of the ASIC Act (ss 203 – 223) provides for the establishment of a Companies Auditors Disciplinary Board. The Board is an independent statutory body established under s 203 of the ASIC Act.

The primary role of the Board is to act as an expert disciplinary tribunal, whose role is necessarily restricted to the review and assessment of auditors and audit companies. The Board can hold hearings to consider applications for the cancellation or suspension of auditors registered under the Corporations Act.

Part 11 of the ASIC Act (Divs 1 and 2, ss 203 – 223) governs the conduct of the Companies Auditors Disciplinary Board, including:

- Membership of the Board – Pt 11, Div 1, s 203
- Functions and powers of the Board – Pt 11, Div 1, s 204
- Meetings of the Board – Pt 11, Div 1, ss 210 and 210B
- Hearings conducted by the Board – Pt 11, Div 2, s 216
- Power of the Board to summon witnesses and gather evidence – Pt 11, Div 2, s 217.

Chapter 3

ASIC DISCRETIONS IN PERFORMING ITS ROLE

This chapter discusses the discretions afforded to ASIC to assist it in performing its role as a corporate and financial services regulator.

¶3-000 ASIC Discretions

In performing its role, ASIC is provided with several discretions under both the ASIC Act and the Corporations Act. Exercising those discretions may involve ASIC issuing legislative instruments, individual instruments, regulatory guides, consultation papers, reports and information sheets.

Legislative instruments or individual instruments

These instruments exempt parties from certain provisions of, or modify the operation of, the Corporations Act. Legislative instruments carry the force of law and are made under specific provisions of the Corporations Act which confer powers on ASIC and permit ASIC to create, modify and remove legal rights: *ASIC v DB Management Pty Ltd & Ors* (2000) 18 ACLC 166. Prior to 2015, legislative instruments were referred to as class orders.

Refer to ¶3-010 below for further information.

Regulatory guides, consultation papers, reports and information sheets

Although these documents can be influential, they do not carry the force of law and do not substitute for the statute (be that the ASIC Act or the Corporations Act). Indeed, policy guidance should be treated with caution, especially in the case of complex commercial matters: *Westchester Financial Services Pty Ltd v Australian Securities Commission* (1998) 16 ACLC 1,281 (AAT); *In the matter of Brisbane Broncos Ltd (No 3)* (2002) 20 ACLC 1, (which relates specifically to the Takeovers Panel).

Hence, regulatory guides and consultation papers, etc *express* policy, whilst legislative instruments actually *implement* that policy. It is important to note that ASIC's discretionary power to make a legislative instrument, in regard to a certain matter, is not limited in any way by ASIC's policy on that matter: *Otter Gold Mines Ltd v ASC* (1997) 15 ACLC 387.

Refer to ¶3-020 below for further information.

¶3-010 ASIC Legislative Instruments

ASIC has the power to exempt parties, corporations and registered schemes from, or modify the operation of, certain provisions of the Corporations Act. This power is found in the relevant Part or Chapter of the Corporations Act. For example:

- Sections 340 and 341 – Financial reporting
- Sections 340A and 341A – Foreign passport funds
- Section 601QA – Managed investment schemes
- Section 655A – Takeovers
- Section 741 – Fundraising
- Section 1020F – Product Disclosure Statements

ASIC typically uses its exemption and modification powers in response to requests for relief from parties who may be experiencing difficulties in complying with the legislation. The extent to which ASIC can use its powers to create rights and impose liabilities on parties is a question which may involve constitutional issues relating to the separation of powers doctrine and the power of the legislature to delegate law-making powers to administrative bodies.

It is important to note that ASIC does not possess modification and exemption powers in respect of every Chapter or Part of the Corporations Act. For example, ASIC does not have any legislative instrument power in relation to the external administration provisions in Chapter 5 of the Corporations Act.

Commencement of legislative instruments

When it comes to the commencement of legislative instruments, there are 3 rules:

(a) Legislative instruments usually commence on the date on which they are executed by the appropriate ASIC delegate. Because legislative instruments enable ASIC to create, modify and remove legal rights, they do not ordinarily have retrospective effect

(b) In the following 2 cases, a legislative instrument may come into effect on a future date, indicated in the text of the instrument itself.

  - Firstly – Where ASIC wishes to provide industry with sufficient time to adjust to the practical effect of the new instrument.
  - Secondly – Where there is a significant period of time between the enactment of an amending Act and its date of commencement. ASIC can make instruments based on a conferral of powers by sections of an amending Act which are yet to commence, provided that the date of effect of the instrument is the date of commencement of the amending Act, ss 4(1) and (2A)(c) of the *Acts Interpretation Act 1901 (Cth)*.

(c) A legislative instrument will commence in accordance with s 12 of the *Legislation Act 2003 (Cth)*; this is usually on a day specified in the instrument itself, which is generally on the day, or some date after, it is registered on the Federal Register of Legislation. Section 56 of the Legislation Act provides that any requirement for notification of the instrument in the *Gazette* is satisfied if the instrument is registered on the Federal Register of Legislation.

¶3-020 ASIC Regulatory Guides, Consultation Papers, Reports and Information Sheets

ASIC provides legal practitioners with an abundance of guidance documents on how ASIC exercises its discretions in performing its role. These documents include policies on both general and specific discretions.

ASIC's guidance documents fall into 4 broad categories:

1. Regulatory Guides (RG) – These documents provide guidance to regulated entities by explaining when and how ASIC exercises specific powers under legislation (primarily the Corporations Act), how ASIC interprets the law and the principles underlying ASIC's approach to its role. Regulatory guides also offer practical guidance; for example, describing a process such as applying for a licence or providing practical examples of how regulated entities can meet their obligations
2. Consultation Papers (CP) – These documents seek feedback from industry stakeholders on policy matters which ASIC is considering, such as proposed relief, policy amendments or regulatory guidance
3. Reports (REP) – These documents describe ASIC compliance with certain obligations or provisions of the legislation, relief activity or the results of a particular research project
4. Information sheets (INFO) – These documents provide guidance and assistance to industry on a specific ASIC process, compliance issue or area of law. They may also provide detailed guidance on a particular topic. However, Information Sheets do not necessarily consider all issues or list all obligations.

ASIC Regulatory Guides

ASIC regulatory guides on specific discretions are noted in this book. Regulatory guides on ASIC's general approach to discretions are listed below:

- Regulatory Guide 21: *How ASIC charges fees for relief applications* – This guide sets out how ASIC fees are calculated for applications to ASIC to exercise its discretionary powers
- Regulatory Guide 51: *Applications for relief* – This guide sets out ASIC's policy for processing applications for relief from the Corporations Act
- Regulatory Guide 57: *Notification of rights of review* – This guide sets out the circumstances under which ASIC must notify parties of their right to have an ASIC decision reviewed by the Administrative Appeals Tribunal
- Regulatory Guide 92: *Procedural fairness to third parties* – This guide sets out ASIC's policy for third party procedural fairness when considering applications for relief from the Corporations Act
- Regulatory Guide 103: *Confidentiality and release of information* – This guide deals with the disclosure of information obtained by ASIC subject to the exercise of its compulsory powers
- Regulatory Guide 108: *No-action letters* – This guide sets out ASIC's policy regarding statements on which ASIC does not intend to take any regulatory action over certain matters or conduct, be that past or future conduct.

Chapter 4

ASIC'S OTHER ROLES

As discussed in Chapter 1, ASIC's primary role as Australia's corporate regulator requires ASIC to monitor the compliance of corporations, financial bodies and registered investment schemes with the Corporations Act. ASIC is granted certain powers under the Corporations Act to permit it to carry out this role.

However, ASIC's role also requires the administration of additional Acts of the Commonwealth. This chapter discusses the additional roles for which ASIC is responsible.

Section 12A of the ASIC Act lists the following Acts which confer additional functions and powers on ASIC:

- *ASIC Supervisory Cost Recovery Levy Act 2017 (Cth)*
- *ASIC Supervisory Cost Recovery Levy (Collection) Act 2017 (Cth)*
- *Business Names Registration (Transitional and Consequential Provisions) Act 2011 (Cth)*
- *National Consumer Credit Protection Act 2009 (Cth)*
- *National Consumer Credit Protection (Transitional and Consequential Provisions) Act 2009 (Cth)*
- *Retirement Savings Accounts Act 1997 (Cth)*
- *Life Insurance Act 1995 (Cth)*
- *Superannuation Industry (Supervision) Act 1993 (Cth)*
- *Insurance Contracts Act 1984 (Cth).*

¶4-000 ASIC's Role in Relation to Australia's Financial System

An underlying theme to ASIC's additional roles is to monitor and promote market integrity and consumer protection in relation to Australia's financial system, s 12A(2) of the ASIC Act. The term "financial system" is necessarily broad and includes banking products, financial advice, superannuation and life insurance. However, ASIC does not necessarily have responsibility for administration of all aspects of the Acts, as listed in s 12A of the ASIC Act; rather, responsibility for the prudential aspects of those Acts is vested in the Australian Prudential Regulation Authority (APRA).

¶4-010 ASIC's Role in Relation to Credit Protection

Under s 239 of the *National Consumer Credit Protection Act 2009 (Cth)*, ASIC has a role in general administration of the **National Consumer Credit Protection regime**. Hence, ASIC administers the national licensing regime established by those Acts under which consumer credit providers are obliged to hold an Australian Credit Licence (ACL). The substantive elements of that licensing regime are that it:

- requires parties who engage in credit activities to, initially, be registered with ASIC, and subsequently to hold an ACL
- imposes entry standards for registration and licensing, and enables ASIC to refuse an application where the applicant fails to meet those standards,
- empowers ASIC to suspend or cancel a licence or registration, or to ban an individual from engaging in credit activities, and
- requires registered parties and licensees to meet ongoing standards of conduct whilst engaging in credit activities.

¶4-020 ASIC's Role in Relation to Business Name Registration

ASIC is responsible for administration of the national **Business Names Register** which is established under the *Business Names Registration Act 2011 (Cth)*. This is a single national business name register which provides online registration for both Australian Business Numbers (ABNs) and business names.

¶4-030 ASIC's Role in Relation to Payment Systems

ASIC has a role in monitoring and promoting market integrity and consumer protection in relation to payment systems, s 12A(3) of the ASIC Act. The Reserve Bank of Australia (RBA) defines "payments system" as arrangements which permit consumers, businesses and other organisations to transfer funds usually held in an account at a financial institution to one another.

When it comes to payment systems, under ss 12A(3) and (4) of the ASIC Act, ASIC is responsible for:

- endorsing the adoption of approved industry standards and codes of practice, s 12A(3)(a) of the ASIC Act
- promoting community awareness of payment system issues and the protection of consumer interests, via regular reporting, and
- fostering sound relationships between financial institutions and consumers, by monitoring the operation of, and compliance with, industry standards and codes of practice, s 12A(3)(d) of the ASIC Act.

Under s 12A(5)(a) of the ASIC Act, ASIC can also make recommendations to the Minister on legislative changes, to any of the laws as listed in s 12A(1) of the ASIC Act, in order to overcome any issues encountered by it in performing its functions and powers. Section 12A(5)(b) permits ASIC to make any recommendations to the Minister as it sees fits, in regard to its roles under ss 12A(2) and (3) of the ASIC Act – being the monitoring and promotion of market integrity and consumer protection in relation to Australia's financial system and payments systems.

Section 12A(6) of the ASIC Act confers a broad power on ASIC to do whatever is necessary for, or in connection with, or reasonably incidental to the performance of its roles. This confers a wide discretionary power on ASIC, beyond just that as mandated by the legislation.

¶4-040 ASIC's Expanded Role following the Banking Royal Commission

The Royal Commission into Misconduct in the Banking, Superannuation and Financial Services Industry (Banking Royal Commission) was established on 14 December 2017. The Commission was headed by the Honourable Kenneth Madison Hayne AC QC and is often referred to as the "Hayne Royal Commission". The Commission delivered its final report to Parliament on 1 February 2019.

The report was largely scathing in its assessment of conduct within the financial services industry. In particular, the Commission uncovered explicit examples of financial institutions taking advantage of those more vulnerable clients, through increased fees (even for deceased clients), complex financial products combined with a lack of explanation or assistance and unethical practices such as the hawking of financial products and add-on insurances.

As a result of the Banking Royal Commission's investigation and report, several legislative reforms were introduced to combat the issues as identified by the Banking Royal Commission. The *Financial Sector Reform (Hayne Royal Commission Response) Act 2020 (Cth)* commenced on 1 January 2021.

The Amending Act made amendments to the following legislation:

- *The ASIC Act*
- *The Corporations Act*
- *The Competition and Consumer Act 2010 (Cth)*
- *The National Consumer Credit Protection Act 2009 (Cth)*
- *The National Consumer Credit Protection (Transitional and Consequential Provisions) Act 2009 (Cth)*
- *The Australian Prudential Regulation Authority Act 1998 (Cth)*
- *The Life Insurance Act 1995 (Cth)*
- *The Superannuation Industry (Supervision) Act 1993, (SIS Act)*
- *The Insurance Contracts Act 1984 (Cth)* and
- *The Insurance Act 1973 (Cth).*

However, the focus of this publication is on the amendments to the ASIC Act which are contained in Schedules 3, 4, 9 (Pt 2) and 12 of the Amending Act.

New deferred sales model for add-on insurance

Schedule 3 of the Amending Act legislates the Federal Government's response to Recommendation 4.3 from the Banking Royal Commission concerning a deferred sales model for add-on insurance products. Specifically, the recommendation stated:

> *"A Treasury-led working group should develop an industry-wide deferred sales model for the sale of any add-on insurance products, except policies of comprehensive motor insurance. The model should be implemented as soon as is reasonably practicable."*

The reforms to the ASIC Act seek to ensure that clients are provided with sufficient time to make informed purchasing decisions when it comes to add-on insurance products. Add-on insurance products are defined as products which are sold together with, or in relation to, the sale of other goods or services (known as the primary product). Typically, the sale of an add-on product comes soon after the sale of the primary product. Under the amendments to the ASIC Act, the add-on insurance deferred sales period is now set at **4 days** from the date on which the client purchased the primary product.

Caps on commissions for vehicle dealers for add-on insurance products

Schedule 4 of the Amending Act legislates the Federal Government's response to Recommendation 4.4 from the Banking Royal Commission concerning a cap on commissions for vehicle dealers and add-on insurance products. Specifically, the recommendation stated:

> *"ASIC should impose a cap on the amount of commission that may be paid to vehicle dealers in relation to the sale of add-on insurance products."*

Hence Sch 4 of the Amending Act imposes a cap on the amount of add-on insurance commissions which may be paid to motor vehicle dealers in relation to the sale of an add-on risk product to clients, as defined in s 12DMC of the ASIC Act. For example, a cap would apply to the commission which may be received by a motor vehicle dealer who is also permitted to sell mechanical breakdown insurance or consumer credit insurance for the sale or lease of a motor vehicle to a client. Refer to s 12DMC of the ASIC Act.

Section 12DMC of the ASIC Act defines an "add-on risk product" as:

> *"An add-on risk product is a financial product that is a facility through which, or through the acquisition of which, a person manages financial risk (within the meaning of subsection 12BAA(5))."*

If a commission is paid which contravenes s 12DMC of the ASIC Act, then the client is entitled to recover the value of the commission, under s 12GFA of the ASIC Act. Contravention of s 12DMC of the ASIC Act, constitutes an offence under s 12GB of the Act.

Under s 12DMC(3) of the ASIC Act, the cap on commissions is determined by ASIC by way of legislative instrument. The methodology for the valuation of a commission is set out in ss 12DMC(5) – (7) of the ASIC Act, whilst s 12DMC(8) of the Act provides that multiple commissions to the same dealer for the same sale are to be treated as one single commission.

Refer to ¶6-040 of this publication, for more detailed information on the new:

- Deferred sales model for add-on insurance
- Cap on commissions to motor vehicle dealers for add-on risk products

Adjustment of ASIC and APRA roles in superannuation

Part 2 of Sch 9 of the Amending Act is concerned with Recommendations 3.8, 6.3, 6.4 and 6.5 from the Banking Royal Commission, each of which are focused on achieving a more harmonised regulatory balance of the superannuation sector between ASIC and APRA. Specifically, the recommendations stated:

- Recommendation 3.8 – The roles of APRA and ASIC with respect to superannuation should be adjusted, as referred to in Recommendation 6.3.
- Recommendation 6.3 – The roles of APRA and ASIC in relation to superannuation should be adjusted to accord with the general principles that:
  - APRA, as the prudential regulator for superannuation, is responsible for establishing and enforcing Prudential Standards and practices designed to ensure that, under all reasonable circumstances, financial promises made by superannuation entities APRA supervises are met within a stable, efficient and competitive financial system
  - As the conduct and disclosure regulator, ASIC's role in superannuation primarily concerns the relationship between Registerable Superannuation Entity (RSE) licensees and individual consumers.

  Effect should be given to these principles by taking the steps in Recommendations 6.4 and 6.5.
- Recommendation 6.4 – Without limiting any powers APRA currently has under the SIS Act, ASIC should be given the power to enforce all provisions in the SIS Act that are, or will become, civil penalty provisions or otherwise give rise to a cause of action against an RSE licensee or director for conduct that may harm a consumer. There should be co-regulation by APRA and ASIC of these provisions.
- Recommendation 6.5 – APRA should retain its current functions, including responsibility for the licensing and supervision of RSE licensees and the powers and functions that come with it, including any power to issue directions that APRA presently has or is to be given.

Hence, the reforms redraw the regulatory functions and responsibilities of APRA and ASIC when it comes to supervision of the superannuation industry.

Part 1 of Sch 9 of the Amending Act amends the SIS Act by expanding ASIC's role in superannuation regulation in order to make ASIC responsible for, inter alia, consumer protection, market integrity, disclosure and record-keeping. Despite the reforms, APRA retains its existing regulatory functions, namely prudential regulation, member outcomes, licensing and supervision of RSE licensees.

Part 2 of Sch 9 of the Amending Act makes the following amendments to the ASIC Act, so as to capture superannuation trustee services for the purposes of the Australian Financial Services Licensee (AFSL) regime.

Firstly, s 12BA(1) of the ASIC Act has been amended by the insertion of the following definitions:

- "registrable superannuation entity" has the same meaning as in the SIS Act.

- "superannuation trustee service" has the same meaning as in Ch 7 of the Corporations Act.

Secondly, s 12BAB(1)(e) of the ASIC Act now has a new subsection (ea) which provides that a "superannuation trustee service" is a "financial service".

Thirdly, s 12GBB(5) of the ASIC Act now provides that, in determining a pecuniary penalty, the Court must take into account all relevant matters, including:

> "(e) in the case of a contravention by the trustee of a registrable superannuation entity – the impact that the penalty under consideration would have on the beneficiaries of the entity".

Finally, s 93C of the ASIC Act now has a subsection (2) which provides that:

> "(2) If:
>
> (a) a person commits an offence against this Act in the person's capacity as trustee of a registrable superannuation entity, and
>
> (b) the penalty applicable to the offence is, or includes, a fine,
>
> then, in determining the fine for the offence, the court must take into account the impact that the fine under consideration would have on the beneficiaries of the entity."

Statutory obligation on ASIC and APRA to cooperate

Schedule 12 of the Amending Act contains the following recommendations from the Banking Royal Commission's final report:

- Recommendation 6.9 – Statutory obligation on ASIC and APRA to co-operate and share information, and
- Recommendation 6.11 – Formalising ASIC meeting procedures, including the times and places of ASIC meetings, the quorum required, who is permitted to preside, how voting is to occur and the passing of resolutions without ASIC meetings.

As the primary regulator for financial institutions, ASIC's role was necessarily expanded under the ASIC Act, to enhance its power in dealing with financial misconduct.

As a result, s 12AA was added to the ASIC Act, which set out ASIC's obligations for cooperation with APRA. Similar cooperation obligations for APRA have been inserted in section 10A of the *Australian Prudential Regulation Authority Act 1998 (Cth).*

Part 6A (s 122B – 122E) was also added to the ASIC Act. These sections set out ASIC's obligations to provide information to APRA. This includes:

Section 122B of the ASIC Act, provides that APRA may request certain information or documents from ASIC. Such a request from APRA must be in writing and can be amended or withdrawn by APRA (again in writing).

Section 122C of the ASIC Act prescribes that ASIC must comply with a s 122B request as soon as practicable. However, ASIC is not obliged to comply with the request if the ASIC Chairperson personally determines in writing that complying with the request would compromise the proper functioning of ASIC, s 122C(4) of the ASIC Act.

Section 122D of the ASIC Act sets out the broad scope of information and documents referred to in s 122B(1)(a). Despite the wide range of information and documents covered by s 122D of the ASIC Act, ss 122D(4) and (5) of the ASIC Act exclude the following:

- Information or documents concerning the internal administrative functioning of ASIC,
- Information or documents disclosing matters in respect of which ASIC, or any other party, has claimed legal professional privilege,
- Information or documents of a kind specified in the regulations, or
- Information or documents communicated to a member, or staff member, in accordance with s 68(p) of the *Telecommunications (Interception and Access) Act 1979 (Cth).*

Section 122E of the ASIC Act sets out an obligation on ASIC to inform APRA if it believes material breach of a legislative provision has occurred, where APRA has general administration of that provision.

Refer to Chapter 6 for more detailed information on ASIC's significant role in regulating unconscionable conduct and facilitating consumer protection in the financial services sector.

Chapter 5

ASIC'S SUPERVISORY COST RECOVERY ROLE

ASIC has a role in managing its regulatory and supervisory costs. It does this through the imposition of levies and fees for service. This chapter discusses ASIC's role in determining, imposing and enforcing levies on the corporate and financial services industry.

¶5-000 Introduction

ASIC's regulatory costs are recovered from all industry sectors, as regulated by ASIC, through annual levies and fees for specific services. These include industry levies and costs recovered directly from an entity who has requested that ASIC carry out specific regulatory activities (fees for service).

Industry levies are imposed annually and are aimed at recovering ASIC's regulatory costs for the previous financial year. All corporations, which are regulated by ASIC, contribute towards ASIC's regulatory costs incurred in the previous financial year. Some corporations pay a flat levy, with the cost of regulating a sub-sector shared equally among the entities operating in that sub-sector. Other corporations pay a graduated levy, with the entity's size or business activity determining its share of costs.

Part of ASIC's role is to consult annually on industry levies. It does this through its Cost Recovery Implementation Statement (CRIS). The CRIS ensures that ASIC's costs are clear and transparent and provides information on how the cost of ASIC's regulatory activities will be recovered from each industry sub-sector. The CRIS also includes ASIC's forecast of the work it will undertake for each sub-sector for each financial year and what it will cost to carry out that work. It also provides valuable information on the actual expenses ASIC incurred in the previous year and explains any material variation as compared to the estimates. Copies of a CRIS for a particular financial year are available to download from ASIC's website.

¶5-010 Industry Sectors and Sub-Sectors

The ASIC Supervisory Cost Recovery Levy Regulations 2017 (Cth) prescribe the following 6 sectors and 48 sub-sectors:

1. Corporate sector – with 6 sub-sectors
2. Deposit-taking and credit sector – with 6 sub-sectors
3. Investment management, super and related services sector – with 7 sub-sectors
4. Financial advice sector – with 4 sub-sectors
5. Market infrastructure and intermediaries sector – with 22 sub-sectors
6. Insurance sector – with 3 sub-sectors

¶5-020 Levy Types and ASIC's Role in Calculating Levies

Detailed information on how ASIC calculates levies is available in the ASIC Supervisory Cost Recovery Levy Regulations 2017 (Cth).

Flat levy

A flat levy divides the total cost of regulating a sub-sector equally among the entities operating in that sub-sector. In some sub-sectors, an entity's size or level of business activity will determine the level of risk and regulatory effort required from ASIC and hence the levy charged.

Graduated levy

A graduated levy is calculated by dividing ASIC's regulatory costs for a sub-sector among entities based on the relevant metric and can be made up of (i) a minimum levy, and (ii) a variable levy component. Under the graduated levy, all entities in a sub-sector must pay (i) the minimum levy, and (ii) the variable component, based on each entity's share of relevant activity within the sub-sector. If an entity holds more than one licence or registration (for example, if an entity is both a superannuation trustee and a listed company) then the levy relevant for each sub-sector is payable.

Minimum levy

A minimum levy is an estimate of ASIC's costs of undertaking stakeholder engagement, policy advice, guidance, education and a portion of ASIC's capital expenditure allowance.

Variable levy

ASIC's remaining regulatory costs for the sub-sector are recovered through the variable levy component. This is driven by ASIC's enforcement and surveillance activities for each sub-sector and can vary significantly depending on the conduct and behaviour of industry participants.

¶5-030 Overview of the Process and ASIC's Role

Entities regulated by ASIC, must register and maintain contact details on the ASIC Regulatory Portal. An entity may also be required to submit business activity metrics via the portal between July and September each year. ASIC uses this information to calculate each entity's regulatory costs for the sectors in which they operate. ASIC then issues levy invoices to regulated entities.

The following entities pay little, or no, regulatory costs to ASIC, as detailed below:

- **Small proprietary limited companies** – These entities will pay only a small increase in their annual review fee. However, if the company is part of one of ASIC's other regulated populations, it must submit contact details and business activity metrics in the ASIC Regulatory Portal.
- **Registered charities** – If a charity is registered with the Australian Charities and Not-for-profits Commission (ACNC), as at 30 June each year, it will be excluded from ASIC industry funding obligations.

Chapter 6

ASIC'S ROLE IN REGULATING UNCONSCIONABLE CONDUCT AND CONSUMER PROTECTION IN FINANCIAL SERVICES

One of ASIC's most imperative roles is in regulating unconscionable conduct and facilitating consumer protection in the financial services industry. This is even more important following the final report of the **Banking Royal Commission**, which was delivered on 1 February 2019, and which was scathing in its review of misconduct within the financial services sector. For further details on the Banking Royal Commission refer to ¶4-040 of this publication.

This chapter discusses what is arguably one of ASIC's most important roles as a regulator of corporate and financial services conduct.

¶6-000 Overview of ASIC's Role

Part 2, Div 2 of the ASIC Act, regulates unconscionable conduct and consumer protection in relation to financial services and confers ASIC with powers to carry out that responsibility. This complements ASIC's role and functions in relation to financial services in Chapter 7 of the Corporations Act. The provisions of Pt 2, Div 2 of the ASIC Act closely mirror provisions in the *Competition and Consumer Act 2010 (Cth)*.

Although ASIC has responsibility for consumer protection in relation to financial services, ASIC has delegated certain powers to the Australian Competition and Consumer Commission (ACCC). In addition, APRA oversees the single licensing and prudential regulatory regime, whilst ASIC remains as the market integrity regulator for the finance industry.

The *Treasury Laws Amendment (Strengthening Corporate and Financial Sector Penalties) Act 2019 (Cth)* introduced a stronger penalty framework for breaches of corporations, credit and financial services laws, including corporate and financial sector misconduct.

Jurisdiction between the ASIC Act and the Competition & Consumer Act

Section 131A of the Competition and Consumer Act states that the Australian Consumer Law (ACL), as contained in Sch 2 of the Competition and Consumer Act, does not apply to financial services and financial products (with the exception of linked credit contracts). Hence:

- it is ASIC's role to enforce the unconscionable conduct and consumer protection provisions of the ASIC Act, which apply to the provision of financial services and financial products, and
- the ACCC enforces the unconscionable conduct and consumer protection provisions of the Competition and Consumer Act, which apply to the provision of goods and services, as well as interests in land.

Hence, different legislation may apply to the same transaction, depending on the facts. In some cases, a commercial activity may attract both jurisdictions. For example, the supply of goods and services (ACCC regulation) may also involve the provision of credit (ASIC regulation). If proceedings are brought by either regulator, the court may need to determine which Act will govern the matter. ASIC and the ACCC can cooperate and delegate power to each other in prosecuting matters under either s 102 of the ASIC Act or s 26(1) of the Competition and Consumer Act: *ACCC v CLA Trading Pty Ltd* [2016] FCA 377. In that case, aspects of the car rental process which related to the supply of services were regulated by ASIC. See also *Enterprise Finance Solutions Pty Ltd v Austec Pty Ltd* [2013] FCA 491.

Under s 12AE(1) of the ASIC Act, the provisions of Part 2, Div 2 of the Act do not exclude or limit the concurrent operation of any law of a State or Territory. Part 2, Div 2 can also operate with common law remedies and remedies available under other statutes, unless expressions to the contrary are indicated, s 12AE(3) of the ASIC Act.

Conduct outside Australia

Section 12AC(1) of the ASIC Act, confirms that the unconscionable conduct and consumer protection provisions under the ASIC Act, can apply to overseas conduct:

- by bodies corporate incorporated, or carrying on business, within Australia
- by Australian citizens, or
- by persons ordinarily resident within Australia.

For the purposes of a claim, the Minister must consent in writing to a claimant relying on conduct outside Australia, ss 12AC(2) and (3) of the ASIC Act. However, the Minister must provide consent unless the overseas conduct was authorised, or it would be against national interest to provide consent, s 12AC(4) of the ASIC Act.

¶6-010 Definitions and Interpretation

Sections 12BA – 12BEA of the ASIC Act contain definitions and interpretation rules for operation of the unconscionable conduct and consumer protection regime of Pt 2, Div 2 of the Act. These definitions are summarised below.

Financial service

This is defined in s 12BAB of the ASIC Act, in terms similar to Pt 7.1, Div 4 of the Corporations Act. Section 12BAB(1AA) states that a "financial product" is a financial service for the purposes of Pt 2, Div 2 of the ASIC Act. Other financial services include the provision:

- by a trustee company of a "traditional trustee company service", ss 12BAB(1A) and (1B) of the ASIC Act and ASIC Regulation 2D
- of a crowd-funding service within the meaning of ss 5, 12BAB(1C) and (1D) of the ASIC Act
- of an unsolicited (off-market) offer to purchase a financial product from another party, where that other party acquired the financial product as a retail client, ASIC Regulation 2C.

Financial product advice

This is defined in s 12BAB(5) of the ASIC Act. This definition excludes documents prescribed by the regulations or a document prepared in accordance with Chapter 7 of the Corporations Act which are typically Financial Services Guides (FSGs), Product Disclosure Statements (PDSs) and Statements of Advice (SoAs). Legal advice is also excluded from the definition under s 12BAB(6) of the ASIC Act. Unlike the Corporations Act, s 12BAB does not distinguish between "personal advice" and "general advice" and does not exclude tax advice (within the meaning of the *Tax Agent Services Act 2009 (Cth)*).

Dealing in a financial product

This is defined in s 12BAB(7) of the ASIC Act. Self-dealing in a financial product is not "dealing" unless the party is an issuer of financial products, s 12BAB(9). Further conduct which is, or is not, dealing in financial products may be prescribed by the regulations, s 12BAB(10).

Makes a market for a financial product

This is defined in s 12BAB(11) of the ASIC Act, in terms similar to s 766D(1) of the Corporations Act.

Operating a registered scheme

This is defined in s 12BAB(4) of the ASIC Act. A registered scheme is a managed investment scheme, registered under s 601EB of the Corporations Act. However, a party does not operate a registered scheme if the party is acting as another party's agent or employee or is winding up the scheme.

Custodial or depository service

This is defined in s 12BAB(12) of the ASIC Act, in terms identical to s 766E(1) of the Corporations Act. Section 12BAB(14) of the ASIC Act lists the exceptions to this definition.

Financial market

This is defined in s 12BAB(15) of the ASIC Act, in terms similar to the terms of s 767A(1) of the Corporations Act. Section 12BAB(16) of the ASIC Act lists the exceptions to this definition.

Clearing and settlement facility

This is defined in s 12BAB(17) of the ASIC Act. Section 12BAB(18) of the ASIC Act lists the exceptions to this definition. A clearing and settlement facility provides a mechanism for parties to meet their obligations in relation to financial product transactions.

Financial product

This is defined in s 12BAA of the ASIC Act. Section 12BAB(1AA) states that a "financial product" is a financial service for the purposes of Pt 2, Div 2 of the ASIC Act, which means consumer protections can apply. The definition of financial product includes:

- Making a financial investment – s 12BAA(4)
- Managing financial risk – s 12BAA(5)
- Making non-cash payments – s 12BAA(6)

Section 12BAA(2) of the ASIC Act states that a **facility** through which parties make financial investments, manage financial risks or make non-cash payments is a financial product, subject to the exceptions listed in s 12BAA(8) which has an overriding function and is similar to s 765A(1) of the Corporations Act.

Section 12BAA(7) of the ASIC Act sets out a list of transactions and facilities which are financial products. This is similar to s 764A of the Corporations Act and includes **credit facilities** under s 12BAA(7)(k). See *Quikfund (Australia) Pty Ltd v Prosperity Group International Pty Ltd (in liq)* [2013] FCAFC 5.

Australian **carbon credits** are financial products for the purposes of Pt 2, Div 2 of the ASIC Act and ASIC Regulation 2BB. However, carbon units are not financial products for the purposes of s 12BAA(7), although the ASIC Act continues to apply to carbon units issued before the "designated carbon unit day".

ASIC Regulation 2BC states that certain tradeable water rights (such as water access and irrigation rights) are not financial products for the purposes of the ASIC Act.

Misleading representations on future matters

These representations are defined in s 12BB of the ASIC Act, in terms identical to s 4 of the ACL. Section 12BB defines representations on future matters as misleading unless a party had reasonable grounds for making the representation. Hence, the burden of proof falls on the party making the representation and evidence must be adduced to support their claim, s 12BB(2). If evidence is adduced, then the burden shifts to the plaintiff.

Section 12BB of the ASIC Act imposes an objective test on the party making a representation. This involves considering common sense questions of fact, degree and circumstances: *CCP Australian Airships Ltd v Primus Telecommunications Pty Ltd* [2004] VSCA 232.

The norm for misleading or deceptive conduct is set out in s 12DA of the ASIC Act. There is no breach of s 12DA if representations on future matters did not eventuate, even if an applicant has relied on them: *Bill Acceptance Corporation Ltd v GWA Ltd* [1983] FCA 269.

Consumer of financial services

This is defined in s 12BC of the ASIC Act, in terms similar to s 3 of the ACL. A party who has acquired financial services for a price not exceeding the prescribed amount, for personal, domestic or household use or for consumption in a small business (between 20 and 100 employees), is a "consumer". The current "prescribed amount" is defined in s 12BC.

Section 12BC(3) of the ASIC Act contains rules for determining the amount payable by a party for services. Section 12BC(4) contains a rebuttable presumption that a party is a consumer of particular services.

Acquisition, supply and re-supply of services

This is defined in s 12BD of the ASIC Act in terms similar to s 11 of the ACL. The term "acquisition" is discussed in *TPC v Tooth & Co Ltd* [1979] HCA 47. "Re-supply" of services includes services re-supplied in substantially the same format, s 12BD(c)(ii) or in an altered form or condition, s 12BD(c)(i).

Asserting a right to payment

This is defined in s 12BEA(1) of the ASIC Act in terms similar to s 10 of the ACL. Section 12BEA(1) sets out circumstances where a party can assert a right to payment for unsolicited financial services or advertisement fees for financial services.

¶6-020 Unfair Contract Terms in Financial Services and ASIC's Role

Sections 12BF–12BM of the ASIC Act, address the use of unfair contract terms in consumer and small business contracts for the supply of financial services. These sections mirror the provisions of Pts 2 – 3 of the ACL.

The provisions are designed to assist ASIC in protecting consumers and small businesses from terms and conditions not disclosed, understood or contemplated, and which are often offered in standard form contracts on a "take it or leave it" basis. The term "contract" takes its ordinary meaning and is subject to the rules of contract law. If a term is not part of a contract, the unfair contract terms regime cannot apply.

Summary of the rules

The principles which can be gleaned from the ASIC provisions regulating unfair contract terms (ss 12BF–12BM of the ASIC Act), are summarised as follows:

1. The rules apply to standard form consumer and small business contracts offered to individuals who acquire financial products or services predominantly for personal, domestic or household use or for small business consumption.
2. There is a rebuttable presumption that a contract under examination in proceedings, under ss 12BF–12BM of the ASIC Act, is a standard form contract.
3. If a term is found to be unfair it will be declared void. If it can be severed from the contract, the remainder of the contract will continue to bind the parties, s 12BF(2). Alternatively, an entire term can be declared void even if only part of the term is unfair: *Director of Consumer Affairs Victoria v Backloads.com Pty Ltd (Civil Claims)* [2009] VCAT 754.
4. **A term will be unfair if *all* of the following tests are met**. The term:
   - would cause significant imbalance in the parties' rights and obligations,
   - is not necessary to protect the legitimate interests of the party who is advantaged, s 12BG(4), and
   - would cause detriment, whether financial or non-financial, to a party. However, a mere likelihood of detriment is insufficient, s 12BG(1)
5. The court's jurisdiction is enlivened by an application, by either ASIC or a party to a contract, for a declaration that a term is unfair. ASIC may intervene in proceedings on behalf of consumers or small businesses as part of a class action.
6. In determining whether a term is unfair, the court must consider whether it is transparent (i.e. concise, legible and accessible) and must consider the term in the context of the whole contract, s 12BG(2).

7. Section 12BH(1) of the ASIC Act provides a non-exhaustive list of examples of terms which *may* be unfair. These can include terms which limit rights, allow one party to unilaterally vary the contract or extend it indefinitely, or permit one party to provide services at their absolute discretion. They may also include any other term as prescribed by the regulations and hence can purposely be broad in its application, s 12BH(1)(n).
8. Unfair contract terms legislation attempts to balance freedom of contract on one hand, with the need to prevent abuse of standard form consumer contracts which are not individually negotiated: *Jetstar Airways Pty Ltd v Free* [2008] VSC 539.
9. In assessing a contract term to be unfair, the "significant imbalance" requirement relates to substantive unfairness of the contract. The requirement is met if a term is so weighted in favour of one particular party: *Director-General of Fair Trading v First National Bank plc* [2002] 1 AC 481.
10. Assessing the impact of a term on the parties may be achieved (in part), by comparing the effect of the contract without the offending term: *Director-General of Fair Trading v First National Bank plc* [2002] 1 AC 481.
11. It is noted that some terms in consumer contracts may be inherently unfair, even if they are notified to the consumer: *Jetstar Airways Pty Ltd v Free* [2008] VSC 539.
12. In considering the contract as a whole, other contract terms should be examined which may counterbalance the offending term in question: *Jetstar Airways Pty Ltd v Free* [2008] VSC 539.

Section 12BF of the ASIC Act governs unfair terms in consumer contracts and small business contracts for the provision of a financial product or financial services. The court's power to declare that a contract term is unfair is found in ss 12GND(1) and (2) of the ASIC Act.

A **small business contract** exists if one contracting party employs less than 20 staff and the contract price is less than $30,000 (for contracts up to one year) or less than $1 million otherwise, s 12BF(4) of the ASIC Act. "Business" includes a not-for-profit business, s 12BA. ASIC Information Sheet 211 – *Unfair contract term protections for small businesses* – provides further guidance on the protections available for small businesses.

Standard form contracts

Section 12BK of the ASIC Act offers some guidance as to whether a particular contract is a standard form contract. The expression takes its ordinary commercial meaning, as explained by the courts. A standard form contract is often defined as a contract which is not individually negotiated but contains the same terms for all transactions of a particular type. It is often offered on a "take it or leave it", "one size fits all" basis. An example is a "tick the box" contract which can be found on many websites.

Section 12BK(1) of the ASIC Act deals with the burden of proof, whilst s 12BK(2) lists factors which a court must take into account when considering whether a particular contract is a standard form contract. These factors include:

- the bargaining power on either party
- which party prepared the contract
- whether discussion or negotiation on the contract was entered into
- whether the terms take into account the particular transaction or characteristics of a party.

Exclusions to the unfair contract terms regime

Section 12BL of the ASIC Act excludes company constitutions, managed investment schemes (including foreign passport funds) and small business contracts (as prescribed by the regulations) from the unfair contracts regime.

Section 12BI of the ASIC Act excludes the following terms from the regime. Terms which:

- define the main subject matter of the contract i.e. concerning existence of the contract itself
- set the upfront price payable under the contract, as disclosed on entering the contract
- are required, or permitted, by a law of the Commonwealth, State or Territory, as a matter of public policy.

ASIC's role in investigating unfair contract terms

Section 13(7) of the ASIC Act was extended to permit ASIC to investigate potential unfair contract terms for contracts dated on or after 26 October 2018, s 316 of the ASIC Act, as inserted by the *Treasury Laws Amendment (Australian Consumer Law Review) Act 2018 (Cth)*. Hence, ASIC's investigative power in relation to unfair contract terms applies to contracts entered into on or after 26 October 2018; however, it does not apply to a contract which is varied or renewed on or after that date, if it was entered into before that date.

Breaches of the unfair contract terms regime

Applying, relying on or enforcing, an unfair term, breaches Pt 2, Div 2 of the ASIC Act. The court may grant an injunction, order compensation, award damages or invalidate the contract, ss 12GA – 12GO. Court orders may also extend to parties who are not a party to the contract, ss 12GNB – 12GNC.

¶6-030 Unconscionable Conduct in Financial Services and ASIC's Role

Sections 12CA – 12CC of the ASIC Act, prohibit unconscionable conduct in the provision of financial services. These provisions closely mirror ss 20 – 22 of the ACL.

What is unconscionable conduct?

It should be noted that there is no general doctrine of unconscionability at common law. It has variously been described as conduct which is harsh, unjust or against conscience by reference to the norms of society, encompassing a disregard of moral judgment or a moral tainting. Notions of justice, fairness, honesty, advantage and vulnerability are key: *Lux Distributors Pty Ltd v ACCC* [2014] HCASL 55. However, it is important to take into account that values, norms and community expectations evolve over time, and what constitutes unconscionable conduct depends largely on the context of a particular case: *Commercial Bank of Australia Ltd v Amadio* [1983] HCA 14, which represents the **current Australian position**, and *Tanwar Enterprises Pty Ltd v Cauchi* [2003] HCA 57.

Increasingly, standard form contracts have become the norm for conducting business. However, these contracts frequently leave consumers in a position of inequality when it comes to dealing with large corporate entities. It is very much a case of "take it or leave it".

The ASIC provisions governing unconscionable conduct

Section 12CB of the ASIC Act prohibits against unconscionable conduct in both business-related and consumer transactions for the supply or acquisition of financial services. Hence, it applies to both suppliers and purchasers and now applies to listed public companies, which were previously excluded from the provisions. However, it does not apply to third parties: *Monroe Topple & Associates v Institute of Chartered Accountants* [2002] FCAFC 197.

Prohibited conduct, under both ss 12CA and 12CB of the ASIC Act, must occur "in trade or commerce". Section 12CB of the Act is drafted broadly to include "possible" supply or acquisition; this ensures that commercial negotiations which failed to eventuate in a transaction, are still brought under the scope of s 12CB. Under s 12CB of the ASIC Act, bringing legal proceedings for unconscionable conduct is not, in itself, considered to be unconscionable.

In determining whether a party has engaged in conduct which is unconscionable, the court must not consider circumstances which were not reasonably foreseeable at the time of the conduct in question, s 12CB(3). Hence, this provision is intended to ensure that parties are not held to an absolute, or impossible, standard of conduct, under which they must be in a position to foresee all probable circumstances.

Section 12CB(4)(a) of the ASIC Act ensures that existing case law on the statutory prohibition against unconscionable conduct, continues to be valid, and that statutory unconscionability can continue to develop independently from the equitable and common law doctrines. Hence, the provision is intended to build on, and not be constrained by, the common law: *ACCC v Radio Rentals* [2005] FCA 1133.

Section 12CB of the ASIC Act is not limited to individual transactions; rather it can apply to a system of conduct or an ongoing pattern of behaviour, s 12CB(4)(b). Unconscionable conduct can also extend beyond the formation of the contract to both its terms and the way in which the contract is carried out, s 12CB(4)(c).

Factors in determining unconscionable conduct

Section 12CC of the ASIC Act provides a non-exhaustive list of factors, for both the supply and acquisition of financial services, which the court may consider in determining if there has been unconscionable conduct, under section 12CB of the Act. However, the presence of one, or more, of these factors is not necessarily, in itself, determinative for a finding of unconscionability: *ACCC v Quantum Housing Group Pty Ltd (No 2)* [2020] FCA 802. These factors include:

1. The relative strengths of bargaining positions of both parties
2. Whether imposed conditions are reasonably necessary to protect the legitimate interests of either party. The court will consider whether onerous terms bear any reasonable correlation to business risks. A contract which is clearly one-sided poses a greater risk to the party seeking to rely on it
3. Whether the contract was explained to, and readily understood by, both parties. This provision catches any element of "unfair surprise" and takes into account the education and literacy capabilities of the parties
4. Whether each party was afforded an opportunity to negotiate the terms. Negotiating opportunities may necessarily be impacted by the bargaining strengths of each party. Standard form "take it or leave it" contracts may present an issue for the party seeking to rely on them
5. The disclosure of any material risks associated with the contract, both before, and after, the contract is made
6. The existence of undue influence, pressure or unfair tactics, such as aggressive bargaining
7. The presence of excessive or inflated contract prices; however, inadequacy of price alone is unlikely to constitute unconscionable conduct
8. Conduct in similar past transactions; however, this must still allow for the realities of commercial flexibility and the fact that even "like" transactions may vary between business settings
9. Whether both parties had received independent legal advice prior to entering a transaction; *Bridgewater v Leahy* [1998] HCA 66; see also *Aboody v Ryan* [2012] NSWCA 395

10. Adherence of the parties to any applicable industry codes, particularly mandatory codes of conduct which bind all market participants
11. Whether both parties acted in good faith; where evidence of good faith, integrity and transparency are legitimate expectations for parties engaged in commercial dealings.

Under s 12CC of the ASIC Act, the time frame for enquiry of unconscionability is not limited to precontract conduct but can also continue once the contract is made. This differs from the common law position as set out in *Wolfe v Permanent Custodians Limited* [2012] VSC 275.

Equitable doctrine of unconscionability

Section 12CA of the ASIC Act is a statutory enactment of the equitable doctrine of unconscionability. Section 12CA(2) states that s 12CA(1) (equitable provision) does not apply to conduct – such as unconscionability in business and consumer transactions – which fall under s 12CB (statutory provision). This codifies the **relationship between the equitable and statutory provisions**.

Equitable jurisdiction to review unconscionable conduct is limited to:

- Heirs & expectants – Where there is a rebuttable presumption of unconscionability, based on the relationship between the parties. For example, an heir to a will in estate planning expects a level of trust based on their connections with the deceased and the estate in question.
- General relief – Where one party is at a special disadvantage due to the particular nuances of the case. For example, advanced age, infirmity or where English is not their native language: *Commercial Bank of Australia v Amadio* [1983] HCA 14; see also *Blomley v Ryan* (1956) 99 CLR 362.

A "special disadvantage or disability" may include poverty, illiteracy, age, infirmity, emotional influence, lack of knowledge and over-dependence: *Louth v Diprose* (1992) 175 CLR 621. Such circumstances do not have to exist at the beginning of a relationship between the parties but may arise subsequently during the course of dealings. However, there must be some factor which elevates a disadvantage to a special disadvantage of which the "stronger" party took advantage. It is also difficult for a corporation to claim unconscionable conduct as this could necessarily imply a breach of ss 180 and 181 of the Corporations Act: *Ridout Nominees Pty Ltd v Commonwealth Bank of Australia* [2003] WASCA 158.

Principles of equitable unconscionability

The following guiding principles can assist ASIC and the courts in determining whether conduct is unconscionable. No one factor alone is definitive of a finding of unconscionability and much will turn on the particular nuances of each case.

1. Relief is not available merely because a bargain is harsh, unfair or unreasonable i.e. something more is required: *Director of Consumer Affairs Victoria v Scully* [2013] VSCA 292; see also *Multiservice Bookbinding Ltd v Marden* [1979] Ch 84

2. Loss is not essential to relief, particularly if the consideration provided in the transaction was adequate: *Commercial Bank of Australia v Amadio* [1983] HCA 14
3. A special disadvantage or disability must be sufficiently evident to the "stronger" party at the time of entering the transaction. This is an objective test based on a reasonable person in similar circumstances. The onus of proof is then on the "stronger" party to show that the transaction was fair, just and reasonable in the circumstances of the case: *Permanent Mortgages Pty Ltd v Vandenbergh* [2010] WASC 10
4. A mere difference in bargaining power between the parties is insufficient, in itself, for a special disability to arise; rather, the conduct of the stronger party must be exploitative or oppressive: *The Bell Group Ltd (in liq) v Westpac Banking Corporation [No 9]* [2008] WASC 239, whilst the "weaker" party must be unable to preserve their interests: *Blomley v Ryan* (1956) 99 CLR 362)
5. Unconscionability must be attributed to a party to the contract and not a third party
6. The object of the doctrine is not to protect parties from what is deemed to be unreasonable, unfair or the consequences of their own mistakes; rather, the doctrine is designed to guard against conduct which is fundamentally harsh or morally flawed.

Other forms of unconscionable conduct

Aside from the equitable doctrine of unconscionability, unconscionable conduct can also arise in the form of undue influence and/or duress:

Undue influence

Undue influence exists where there is a special confidence between 2 parties, and a transaction between those 2 parties serves to disadvantage the "weaker: party. Undue influence may be presumed from a variety of relationships and relates to a more personal type of pressure. The acquisition of independent legal advice will be a strong factor in rebutting the presumption. In *Commercial Bank of Australia v Amadio* [1983] HCA 14, the High Court of Australia distinguished between unconscionable conduct (where a plaintiff has a "special disability"; the focus is on the stronger party taking advantage of this) and undue influence (where a plaintiff's will is overborne; the focus is on the weaker party's assent).

Duress

Duress involves actual violence, or threats of violence, to a party or a close relative of that party. However, mere "commercial pressure" does not constitute duress: *Neale v Bank of Western Australia Ltd; Bank of Western Australia Ltd v Neale* [2014] NSWSC 315. Rather, there must be sufficient "coercion of the will". Hence, a claim of duress will succeed only in extreme circumstances. It is usually linked to commercial circumstances and can be economic duress. Contracts tainted by economic duress can be voidable.

Remedies for unconscionable conduct

Remedies for unconscionable conduct are somewhat limited and may include setting the offending transaction aside. The court may also modify, or partly nullify, unconscionable dealings: *Commercial Bank of Australia v Amadio* [1983] HCA 14. However, damages are not available and relief against third parties may be refused. **Limitations** specific to the equitable doctrine of unconscionability include the fact that:

- the doctrine is likely to be applied only in extreme circumstances,
- the onus of proof on the impacted party, to show unconscionability, is high, and
- the doctrine still largely fails to consider standard form contracts; however, such standard form contracts now have the benefit of the unfair contract terms provisions governing their use.

The doctrine of equitable **estoppel** also prohibits one party (X) from unconscionably departing from an assumption adopted by another party (Y), where Y would suffer detriment if the assumption were not upheld.

¶6-040 Consumer Protection in Financial Services and ASIC's Role

Sections 12DA – 12DN of the ASIC Act, contain several consumer protection measures in relation to the supply of financial services. These provisions include protections against:

- Misleading or deceptive conduct – ss 12DA and 12DF
- False or misleading representations – s 12DB
- Bait advertising – s 12DG
- Referral selling and pyramid selling of financial products – ss 12DH and 12DK
- Accepting payment without supply – s 12DI
- Harassment and coercion – s 12DJ

Misleading or deceptive conduct

Section 12DA(1) of the ASIC Act prohibits misleading and deceptive conduct in relation to financial services. This provision closely mirrors the terms of s 18 of the ACL. **Limitations** to the operation of s 12DA(1) of the ASIC Act, are set out in s 12DA(1A) of the Act. These limitations apply to conduct which falls under the Corporations Act as opposed to the ASIC Act.

Definitions

The definition of "financial service", under s 12BAB(1AA) of the ASIC Act, includes a "financial product". Section 12DA(1) of the ASIC Act refers to "a person". This means that individual employees (as well as corporations) can be held liable for misleading and deceptive conduct: *Motor Trade Finances Prestige Leasing Pty Ltd v Elderslie Finance Group Corporation Ltd and Ors* [2006] NSWSC 1348.

To "engage in conduct" may also include refusing or refraining from carrying out, or engaging in, an act, as defined in s 12BA(2)(c)(i) of the ASIC Act. This covers **silence** as a form of inaction. However, in assessing silence as evidence of misconduct, the circumstances must generally be such as to create a reasonable expectation on a party to speak up: *Demagogue Pty Ltd v Ramensky & Anor* [1992] FCA 557.

The conduct under s 12DA(1) of the ASIC Act, must be "in trade or commerce". The ASIC Act does not define "in trade or commerce". The result is that the expression often derives its meaning from s 51(i) of the Constitution.

The terms "misleading" and "deceptive" are also not defined in the ASIC Act. As a result, their meanings are derived from general principles and an objective test is applied. Hence, a statement may be misleading or deceptive if it results in an ordinary person being led into error. Such a prohibition lies at the root of many torts, such as passing-off, deceit, injurious falsehood or negligent misrepresentation, which all contain the common feature of conduct capable of leading parties into error or which is likely to do so. "Likely" to mislead or deceive means there must be a real chance of a party being led astray, and not a remote possibility: *Global Sportsman Pty Ltd & Anor v Mirror Newspapers Ltd & Anor* [1984] FCA 180.

The prohibition against misleading or deceptive conduct

Knowledge or intention on the part of the defendant i.e. a **mental element**, is not required for a breach of s 12DA of the ASIC Act. Hence, this ensures that conduct such as innocent misrepresentation is caught under the provision. However, even if there was intention to mislead or deceive another party, there is no breach of s 12DA of the Act unless the conduct *actually* misleads or deceives that other party. Additionally, a party does not necessarily breach s 12DA of the ASIC Act by being "involved" in another party's breach of the section: *ASIC v Dover Financial Advisers Pty Ltd (No 2)* [2019] FCA 2151.

Section 12BB of the ASIC Act defines **representations on future matters** as misleading unless a party had reasonable grounds for making the representation. However, **puffery** (which is undue exaggeration or excessive praise), by its very nature, is not misleading or deceptive.

A plaintiff does not have to show **loss or damage** for a breach of s 12DA of the ASIC Act to have occurred. However, if the plaintiff is seeking to recover damages, then they must necessarily show that their loss was caused by the defendant's misconduct and that there was an element of **reliance** on this misconduct. However, this right of recovery does not automatically follow a breach of s 12DA of the ASIC Act.

A plaintiff's own negligence – for example in failing to mitigate their loss – does not protect a defendant from liability. However, s 12GF(1B) of the ASIC Act provides **proportionate liability** for a breach of s 12DA of the Act, if it can be shown that a plaintiff failed to take reasonable care, which in turn contributed to their loss or damage.

Discretionary factors in assessing misconduct

In assessing conduct as misleading or deceptive, the courts may look to the factors as listed below. However, no one factor alone is definitive of a finding of misleading or deceptive conduct; rather much will turn on the individual circumstances of each case.

1. The effect of the **conduct as a whole**, which could include inaction or silence: *Butcher v Lachlan Elder Realty Pty Ltd* [2004] HCA 60; see also *Miller & Associates Insurance Broking Pty Ltd v BMW Australia Finance Ltd* [2010] HCA 31. Looking at conduct as a whole, and not in isolation, is particularly prevalent in the advertising industry in the context of creating a false impression.
2. Evidence that a party has in fact formed an erroneous conclusion. Such proof is persuasive, but not essential. Conduct may also have a capacity to mislead even if it has not yet occurred.

3. Why a proven misconception has arisen; this is essential to show that a plaintiff has indeed been led into error as a direct result of the misleading or deceptive conduct: *Taco Company of Australia Inc & Anor v Taco Bell Pty Ltd & Ors* [1982] FCA 136. It is irrelevant that the plaintiff could have ascertained the true situation by further inquiry: *Collins Marrickville Pty Limited v Henjo Investments Pty Limited & Ors* (1987) 72 ALR 601.

4. It is prudent to measure the alleged offending conduct against some **standard**. However, standards may vary. Hence, conduct to which the public at large is exposed is subject to a stricter standard and must be broader to account for those less educated or who are more easily influenced. Conduct can still be misleading or deceptive even if it fails to deceive those who are more astute or who have special knowledge, although in all cases the "reasonable" person is still the overriding consideration: *Parkdale Custom Built Furniture Pty Ltd v Puxu Pty Ltd* [1982] HCA 44.

5. **Confusion** *may* result in a party being misled or deceived but is not determinative of it: *Taco Company of Australia Inc & Anor v Taco Bell Pty Ltd & Ors* [1982] FCA 136.

6. **Opinions** and testimonials are, by their very nature, subjective. Hence, in order to avoid breach of s 12DA of the ASIC Act, a party expressing an opinion must have some sound basis for doing so. This is particularly important where expert testimony is adduced as part of the evidence in proceedings.

7. **Ambiguity** in conduct or statements will contravene s 12DA of the ASIC Act if any of the possible meanings are misleading or deceptive. This is the case even if a non-misleading meaning is the more obvious one to be adopted in the circumstances.

8. **Qualifying statements, disclaimers and corrections** must be sufficient to dispel any incorrect conclusions. Issues may arise as to the timing of qualifying statements, where the original conduct may remain unqualified, even for a short time, and hence still breaches s 12DA of the ASIC Act. In general, disclaimers have been found to be ineffective for a defendant to evade liability.

9. **Professional advice** "in trade or commerce" may breach s 12DA of the ASIC Act, despite any professional liability insurance.

10. The particular issue of the **misconduct of financial institutions** came under increased scrutiny following the Banking Royal Commission.

The court has the final discretion on whether the conduct in question breaches s 12DA of the ASIC Act, and the test is objective. A plaintiff may also initiate an action for misleading or deceptive conduct under the common law and hence have a choice of remedies available to them.

Misrepresentation

Section 12DB(1) of the ASIC Act prohibits false or misleading representations, in the supply or promotion of financial services, in any of the 10 circumstances as listed under ss 12DB(1)(a) – (j) of the Act. Section 12DB(1) of the ASIC Act closely mirrors s 29 of the ACL. **Limitations** to the operation of s 12DB(1) of the ASIC Act are set out in s 12DB(2) of the Act. These limitations apply to conduct which falls under the Corporations Act as opposed to the ASIC Act.

Definitions

Representations must be made "in trade or commerce". The expression "in connection with" means that there must be a sufficient nexus between the supply of financial services and the alleged representation. The term "representation" is not defined in the ASIC Act. Hence, its meaning is derived from general principles.

The prohibition against misrepresentation

Silence may constitute a false representation as to services, but only where the particular circumstances of the case make it necessary for a defendant to clarify, or supply, information in order to avoid a plaintiff being misled: *Ryan & Ors v Great Lakes Council & Ors* [1999] FCA 177.

Disclaimers of liability for false trading descriptions may be effective in protecting against liability. However, any such disclaimers must be as bold, precise and compelling as the trade description itself and be brought to the attention of consumers: *Norman v Burnett* [1974] 3 All ER 351. Any **corrective advertising** should also match the breadth and extent of the original campaign; otherwise it may be missed.

A false representation may be established under s 12DB(1) of the ASIC Act without intention, knowledge, negligence or recklessness on the part of the defendant. Hence, **no mental element** is required: *ASIC v Hobbs* [2012] NSWSC 1276.

Section 12DC(1) of the ASIC Act prohibits false or misleading representations in relation to financial products which involve interests in land.

Section 12DD(1) of the ASIC Act requires a cash price for financial services be provided if only part of the consideration for the services is disclosed. The provision is aimed at financial service providers who induce clients on board by advertising low deposits without disclosing the total price payable. Hence, section 12DD(1) of the Act essentially catches "**part-payments**": *ACCC v Dell Computer Pty Ltd* [2002] FCAFC 434. The section excludes securities within the meaning of Chapter 6 of the Corporations Act which governs takeovers.

Factors in assessing misrepresentations

Sections 12DB(1)(a) – (j) of the ASIC Act list circumstances under which a court may declare a representation to be false or misleading. These include representations as to:

- **Standard** – Under s 12DB(1)(a) of the ASIC Act, services should be of a particular quality, value or grade. The term "standard" extends beyond official standards as imposed by industry bodies.
- **Agreements to acquire services** – Section 12DB(1)(b) of the ASIC Act. This may occur where consumers pay for services without their actual knowledge or agreement: *ACCC v Telstra Corp Ltd* [2018] FCA 571, or where payment is asserted by a defendant for services purportedly ordered by a party, perhaps where that party is recently deceased for example.
- **Testimonials, sponsorship, approval, benefits and affiliation** – Sections 12DB(1)(c) – (f) of the ASIC Act. There is a rebuttable presumption that such representations are misleading. The term "sponsorship" implies that a party stands behind, and endorses, a service. A false claim of sponsorship is akin to the tort of passing off. However, the court must be satisfied that a significant number of consumers have been deceived or misled by the alleged sponsorship: *ASIC v Mayfair Wealth Partners Pty Ltd (No 2)* [2021] FCA 247. The term "approval" suggests a degree of reliability or sanction in the services offered, or the facts claimed. The term "affiliation" appears to have a positive link to "approval" or "sponsorship": *McDonald's System of Australia Pty Ltd v McWilliam's Wines Pty Limited* [1979] FCA 109.
- **Price** – Section 12DB(1)(g) of the ASIC Act. "Price" includes a charge of any description, as defined in s 12BA(1) of the ASIC Act. Representations as to price may be made in writing or orally. A price representation cannot subsequently be varied by the vendor at the point of sale. A discounted price must represent a true reduction and not a discount applied to an already inflated product. All charges must be disclosed: *ASIC v Cash King Pty Ltd* [2005] FCA 1429.
- **Need** – Section 12DB(1)(h) of the ASIC Act. This provision is directed towards conduct which creates a mandated or illusory need. The use of terms in promotional materials such as "must" or "need" may contribute towards a finding of misleading representation.
- **Warranty and guarantees** – Section 12DB(1)(i) of the ASIC Act. Warranties and guarantees have been characterised as a "promise". Section 12DB(1)(i) also covers conditions, rights, remedies and implied warranties under s 12ED of the ASIC Act. In drafting warranties, care must be taken not to mislead consumers as to the rights available to them, and not to impose limitations which go against those consumer rights.

Other unfair practices

Offering rebates, gifts, prizes

Section 12DE of the ASIC Act prohibits the practice of offering rebates, gifts, prizes or other free items in connection with the supply or promotion of financial services, where there is no intention to provide such "perks", s 12DE(1)(c) of the Act, or a failure to provide those "perks" within a reasonable time, s 12DE(2A)(c) of the Act. However, there is no breach of s 12DE(2A)(c) of the ASIC Act if the failure was due to an act or omission of another party or some other cause beyond the defendant's control, s 12DE(2B) of the Act, or if the defendant offers, and the plaintiff accepts, a replacement "perk", s 12DE(2C) of the Act. It is not necessary to show intention, knowledge, recklessness or negligence on the part of the defendant. However, the defence of mistake of fact, is available.

Mislead as to the suitability of financial services

Section 12DF of the ASIC Act prohibits conduct which may mislead the public as to the suitability of financial services. Section 12DF of the ASIC Act largely mirrors s 34 of the ACL. Because the prohibition refers to the "public", the conduct must have a broader scope and impact: *ASIC v Westpac Banking Corp (No 2)* [2018] FCA 751. It is not necessary to show intention, knowledge, recklessness or negligence on the part of the defendant. However, the defence of mistake of fact is available.

Bait advertising

Section 12DG(1) of the ASIC Act prohibits bait advertising – that is advertising financial services at a specified price when there are no reasonable grounds to support that price. The aim of bait advertising is to lure prospective clients and obtain leads by "tempting" clients with initial bargains. Section 12DG of the ASIC Act is equivalent to s 35 of the ACL. A party who has engaged in bait advertising must honour the commitment for a reasonable period at reasonable quantities, having regard to the nature of the market, s 12DG(2) of the ASIC Act. It is a defence if the defendant, within a reasonable time, engages another provider to provide the services or provides equivalent services, where those offer(s) are accepted by the plaintiff, section 12DG(3) of the ASIC Act. The s 12DG prohibition applies to all forms of advertisements.

Referral selling

Section 12DH(1) of the ASIC Act prohibits referral selling – that is offering existing clients a rebate or commission in return for referrals of prospective new clients. The prohibition catches only those cases where the benefit to the existing client is dependent upon subsequent sales or introductions. Section 12DH(1) of the ASIC Act is similar to s 49 of the ACL.

Accepting payment without intending to supply

Section 12DI(1) of the ASIC Act prohibits a financial service provider from accepting payment without intending or being able to supply the financial services, as ordered, within the stipulated time or within a reasonable time: *ASIC v Commonwealth Bank of Australia* [2020] FCA 790. Section 12DI(1) of the ASIC Act is similar to s 36 of the ACL. It is not necessary to show intention, knowledge, recklessness or negligence on the part of the defendant in accepting payment. However, the defence of mistake of fact is available.

Harassment and coercion

Section 12DJ(1) of the ASIC Act prohibits physical force, undue harassment or coercion in connection with the supply of, or payment for, financial services. Unlike many of the other prohibitions, there is no requirement for the conduct to be carried out "in trade or commerce". Section 12DJ(1) of the ASIC Act is similar to section 50 of the ACL. "Undue harassment or coercion" will be determined by the courts having regard to the particular facts of each case. "Harassment" means persistent disturbance or torment and may involve applying repeated pressure on a plaintiff. "Coercion" implies force, or threats of force, which impact on a plaintiff's choice or freedom to act: *Hodges v Webb* [1920] 2 Ch 70. Harassment or coercion may involve abusive language and can occur even if a plaintiff fails to acquiesce to the pressure. The conduct may also be directed to a third party such as a relative: *ACCC v McCaskey* [2000] FCA 1037. However, instituting legal proceedings, which are not themselves vexatious, frivolous or an abuse of process, does not constitute undue harassment or coercion.

Pyramid selling of financial products

Section 12DK(1) of the ASIC Act prohibits the pyramid selling of financial products – that is inducing one targeted party to a trading scheme (X) to pay the scheme promoter (Y), where X expects payment, or other benefits, as a result of introducing other parties (Z) to the scheme. It is not necessary to show intention, knowledge, recklessness or negligence on the part of the promoter. However, the defence of mistake of fact is available. The "prospect" of X receiving payment (for introducing new participants) does not have to be a legally enforceable right, s 12DK(4)(a) of the ASIC Act, and that "prospect of payment" may constitute a large part of inducing X, s 12DK(4)(b) of the ASIC Act. Payment to the scheme promoter (Y), can include part-payment, s 12DK(4)(c) of the ASIC Act. Section 12DK(5) of the ASIC Act defines "trading scheme". Pyramid selling constitutes unfair trading because those at the top of the pyramid obtain payment, not from selling services, but from merely selling positions in the pyramid to others. The financial rewards to be gained are also heavily weighted towards recruiting more participants.

Unsolicited credit or debit cards

Section 12DL(1) of the ASIC Act prohibits credit card companies from issuing unsolicited credit or debit cards, except in accordance with s 12DL(2) of the ASIC Act, which includes renewal, replacement or substitution of a card. The aim is to prevent fraud, protect credit ratings and prevent misguided inflation because of readily available credit. Section 12DL of the ASIC Act is similar to s 39 of the ACL. A party must not convert a credit card to a debit card or vice versa in the absence of a written request, s 12DL(4) of the ASIC Act. Credit and debit cards are defined in s 12DL(5) of the ASIC Act. It is not necessary to show intention, knowledge, recklessness or negligence on the part of the defendant in accepting payment. However, the defence of mistake of fact is available.

Asserting a right to payment for unsolicited financial services

Section 12DM(1) of the ASIC Act prohibits a party from asserting a right to payment for unsolicited financial services: *ASIC v Westpac Banking Corporation* [2022] FCA 359. This includes issuing an invoice for unsolicited services, unless that invoice contains a warning to the effect that it is not a bill requiring any payment, s 12DM(1AA) of the ASIC Act. However, neither prohibition applies if the defendant reasonably believes that they have a right to payment, s 12DM(1A) and (1AB) of the ASIC Act, although the defendant bears the onus of proof in this regard. "Unsolicited" is defined in s 12BAA of the ASIC Act, whilst the meaning of "assert a right to payment" is defined in s 12BEA of the Act. Section 12DM of the ASIC Act is similar to s 40 of the ACL and can apply even if the services were not provided to the other party. It is not necessary to show intention, knowledge, recklessness or negligence on the part of the defendant in accepting payment. However, the defence of mistake of fact is available. Section 12DMA of the ASIC Act provides that a party supplied with unsolicited financial services is not liable to pay for them. This section closely mirrors s 42 of the ACL.

Asserting a right to payment for unauthorised advertisements

Section 12DMB(1) of the ASIC Act prohibits a defendant from asserting a right to payment for unauthorised advertisements for financial services relating to a plaintiff, or their profession, unless the defendant knows, or had reasonable cause to believe, that the plaintiff authorised the advertisement. The onus of proof is on the defendant to show "reasonable cause", s 12DMB(6) of the ASIC Act. This prohibition includes issuing an invoice for unauthorised advertisements, unless that invoice contains a warning to the effect that it is not a bill requiring any payment, s 12DMB(2) of the ASIC Act. The plaintiff has a right to recover any payment already made, through court action, s 12DMB(4) of the ASIC Act. Exceptions to the prohibition are listed in s 12DMB(3) of the ASIC Act. Unlike some of the other prohibitions, intention on the part of the defendant must be shown. The meaning of "assert a right to payment" is defined in s 12BEA of the ASIC Act. Section 12DMB of the ASIC Act closely mirrors s 43 of the ACL.

Cap on commissions to motor vehicle dealers for add-on risk products

Section 12DMC(1)(e) of the ASIC Act imposes a cap on commissions payable to motor vehicle dealers for the sale of add-on risk products, such as insurance, to consumers. Pursuant to s 12GFA of the ASIC Act, the consumer can recover the value of any commission already paid which contravenes s 12DMC. The cap is determined by ASIC pursuant to s 12DMC(3) of the ASIC Act. The methodology for determining the value of a commission is set out in ss 12DMC(5) – (7) of the ASIC Act, while s 12DMC(8) of the Act provides that multiple commissions to the same dealer, for the same sale, are to be treated as one commission.

The "information providers" exception

Section 12DN of the ASIC Act provides that the prohibitions in ss 12DA – 12DC and s 12DF of the ASIC Act do not apply to publications by an information provider, s 12DN(5), in the course of carrying on a business of providing information, including by radio or television. Section 12DN of the ASIC Act closely mirrors s 19 of the ACL.

Exceptions to the information providers immunity are outlined in ss 12DN(2) – 12DN(4A) of the ASIC Act and include advertisements; the rationale being that advertising in general should be protected by freedom of the press. The exception to this is where advertisements promote goods or services, where those advertisements can then be subject to scrutiny for misleading or deceptive conduct in connection with the promotion of those goods or services: *ACCC v Channel Seven Brisbane Pty Limited* [2009] HCA 19.

Deferred sales for add-on insurance products

Sections 12DO – 12DZA of the ASIC Act set out a new deferred sales model for add-on insurance, introduced in response to the Banking Royal Commission. ASIC Regulatory Guide 275 (RG 275) – *The Deferred Sales Model for Add-On Insurance* – sets out further guidance on compliance with these sections.

Section 12DO(1)(a) of the ASIC Act defines an "add-on insurance product" as one which is offered to a consumer in connection with a consumer acquiring the principal financial service. It is essentially a contract of insurance, s 12DO(2) of the ASIC Act, which manages the financial risk (within the meaning of s 12BAAA of the ASIC Act) relating to the principal product.

Section 12DP of the ASIC Act sets out a "**deferral period**" for the sale of an "add-on insurance product", as 4 days between when a consumer acquires a principal financial service and when they are offered an add-on insurance product. In offering a consumer an add-on insurance product, the consumer must be given the information referred to in s 12DP(4) of the ASIC Act, and as set out in Appendix 1 to ASIC Regulatory Guide 275 – *The Deferred Sales Model for Add-On Insurance*. This information includes providing the consumer with details on opting-out of receiving information on an add-on insurance product.

During the deferral period, there is a prohibition on selling or offering any further add-on insurance products, ss 12DQ(1) and 12DR(1) of the ASIC Act. There is also a prohibition on offering add-on insurance products if a consumer has indicated they do not want to receive such offers (i.e. opt out), s 12DS(1) of the ASIC Act. Failure to comply with these sections is an offence under s 12GB of the ASIC Act. If an insurance provider breaches s 12DQ of the ASIC Act by selling an add-on insurance product during the deferral period, the consumer is entitled to a full refund of the amount paid for the product, s 12DT(1) of the ASIC Act.

Sections 12DU – 12DY of the ASIC Act set out the following **exceptions** to the deferred sales model for add-on insurance products:

1. Financial advisers – Where a financial adviser sells the add-on insurance in the course of providing personal advice in accordance with the best interests duty under Pt 7.7A, Div 2 of the Corporations Act, s 12DU of the ASIC Act
2. Product intervention order – Where the add-on insurance is the subject of a product intervention order under Pt 9.7A of the Corporations Act, s 12DV of the ASIC Act

3. Compulsory motor vehicle insurance – Where the add-on insurance applies to a contract for a party who owns, or has use of, a motor vehicle and where the cover is for loss of, or damage to, the motor vehicle or property resulting from an accident, fire, theft or malicious acts, s 12DW of the ASIC Act
4. Regulations – Where add-on insurance is exempted by Pt 2A of the ASIC Regulations, s 12DX of the ASIC Act
5. ASIC – Where add-on insurance is exempted by ASIC itself, s 12DY of the ASIC Act.

¶6-050 Conditions and Warranties in Consumer Transactions and ASIC's Role

Sections 12EA – 12ED of the ASIC Act imply certain conditions and warranties into contracts for the supply of financial services to a consumer. These provisions are only available to parties to the contract and are similar to those implied at common law.

Definitions

A "condition" is a term which goes to the very essence of the contract, breach of which gives rise to rescission of the contract and a right to compensation.

A "warranty" is of lesser importance, breach of which gives rise to damages but not the right to reject the services or terminate the contract: *Oscar Chess Ltd v Williams* [1957] 1 WLR 370; [1957] 1 All ER 325.

Conflict of laws

Section 12EA of the ASIC Act prevents parties "contracting out" of the implied conditions and warranties of ss 12EA – 12ED of the ASIC Act by claiming that a foreign law governs the contract. Section 12EA of the ASIC Act closely mirrors s 67 of the ACL. It expressly overrides a contractual choice of law clause: *Insight Vacations Pty Ltd v Young* [2010] NSWCA 137; *Laminex (Aust) Pty Ltd v Coe Manufacturing Co* [1999] NSWCA 370.

Exclusions or modifications of implied conditions and warranties are void

Section 12EB(1) of the ASIC Act provides that a contract term is void if it attempts to exclude, restrict or modify the provisions of ss 12EA – 12ED of the ASIC Act, or any rights or liabilities conferred by those provisions. Hence, the section prevents attempts to limit the operation of ss 12EA – 12ED of the ASIC Act as to the terms of a contract and the remedies which are available. However, it does not save an offending term to the extent of any inconsistency. This means that a term may be void in its entirety, even if it only part of the term offends.

Limitation of liability

Section 12EC(1) of the ASIC Act permits a financial services provider to limit its liability, to the replacement, or cost of replacing the services, in some circumstances, unless it is unfair or unreasonable for the provider to rely on that term of the contract which limits liability, s 12EC(2) of the ASIC Act.

Section 12EC(3) of the ASIC Act sets out the following matters, which a court *must* consider, in determining whether it fair or reasonable for a provider to rely on a term of the contract which limits liability:

(a) the relative strength of the bargaining positions of each party, taking into account alternative sources of supply

(b) whether the consumer was induced to accept the term or had an alternative option to acquire the services

(c) whether the consumer was aware of the term, or ought reasonably to have known of it, having regard to any previous dealings between the parties.

If the whole purpose of the supply of services is frustrated, it would generally be unfair to permit a defendant to limit liability: *Indico Holdings Pty Ltd v TNT Australia Pty Ltd* (1990) 41 NSWLR 281.

Implied warranties in relation to the supply of financial services

Section 12ED(1) of the ASIC Act implies the following warranties into contracts for the supply of financial services to a consumer. These provisions warrant that:

- services will be rendered with due care and skill
- materials will be reasonably fit for the purpose for which they are supplied: *Gharibian v Propix Pty Ltd t/a Jamberoo Recreational Park* [2007] NSWCA 151
- services and materials will be reasonably fit for a purpose as notified by the consumer; however, a consumer's more general, or broader, statement of goals is unlikely to be sufficient for this purpose: *Jamieson v Westpac Banking Corp* [2014] QSC 032.

Actual knowledge of a defect in the services will prevent a consumer from relying on a warranty: *Bethune v QConn Pty Ltd (t/a Case Adelaide)* [2002] FCA 1485.

The **remedy** for contravention of s 12ED of the ASIC Act is breach of contract and not damages. Contracts of insurance are **excluded** from the provisions, s 12ED(3) of the ASIC Act. Section 12ED(2A) of the ASIC Act preserves the operation of State or Territory laws to the extent of any inconsistency.

¶6-060 ASIC's Role in Enforcement and Remedies

Sections 12GA – 12GO of the ASIC Act permit ASIC to institute proceedings for a range of **civil penalties** for breach of Div 2 of the ASIC Act and provide for **criminal prosecutions**. These sections are summarised as follows:

Offences

Section 12GB of the ASIC Act is the primary offence provision, creating offences for breach of the consumer protection provisions, except s 12DA of the ASIC Act (relating to misleading or deceptive conduct). A party may also be guilty of an offence if they aid, abet or counsel another party to breach the provisions (**accessorial liability**) and parts of the Criminal Code will apply, ss 12GB(1A) and (1B) of the ASIC Act. Accessorial liability requires knowledge on the part of the defendant: *Cassidy v NRMA Health Pty Ltd* [2002] FCA 1228.

Civil penalties

Sections 12GBA – 12GBCP of the ASIC Act impose civil penalties. These provisions have been significantly amended by the *Treasury Laws Amendment (Strengthening Corporate and Financial Sector Penalties) Act 2019 (Cth).* Sections 12GBA(1) and 113(2) of the National Credit Code ("Penalty orders") secure compliance with the relevant provisions of the regime, with the court to determine an appropriate penalty based on the circumstances of the case: *ASIC v Rent 2 Own Cars Australia Pty Ltd (No 2)* [2022] FCA 491.

Pecuniary penalties

Section 12GBB of the ASIC Act allows ASIC to apply for the imposition of pecuniary penalties, as an alternative to criminal prosecution. Section 12GBCB of the ASIC Act defines a pecuniary penalty as a debt payable to the Commonwealth which may be enforced in civil proceedings as if it were a judgment debt. An application must be made within 6 years of the alleged contravention, s 12GBB(2) of the ASIC Act. Section 12GBB(5) of the ASIC Act sets out the factors which a court must consider in determining the amount of a pecuniary penalty. Section 12GBCA of the ASIC Act determines the value of a pecuniary penalty: *ASIC v La Trobe Financial Asset Management Ltd* [2021] FCA 1417. Section 12GBD of the ASIC Act prevents the indemnification of corporate officers for liabilities related to the imposition of pecuniary penalties. This applies to both the original proceedings and any appeal, s 12GBD(2) of the ASIC Act.

Evidence

Under s 12GBCF of the ASIC Act the **rules of evidence** and procedure will apply in a civil hearing for a declaration of a contravention, a pecuniary penalty order or a relinquishment order. Evidence provided in civil proceedings is not admissible in related criminal proceedings except in relation to falsity of the evidence given by the individual in proceedings for a pecuniary penalty order, s 12GBCK of the ASIC Act.

Burden of proof

The defendant in proceedings for a declaration of contravention, pecuniary penalty order, relinquishment order or any other order bears the onus of proving any applicable exception, exemption, excuse, qualification or justification, s 12GBCP of the ASIC Act.

Corporate liability

Section 12GH of the ASIC Act regulates conduct by officers of a corporation for corporate liability. Section 12GH(1) attributes the state of mind of a director, employee or agent of a body corporate, acting in the scope of their authority, to the body corporate. Hence, the conduct of an individual corporate officer may be attributable to the corporation, provided the officer is acting within their authority, s 12GH(2) of the ASIC Act. "State of mind" means knowledge, intention, opinion, belief or purpose, s 12GH(5) of the ASIC Act. Sections 12GH(3) and (4) are drafted in similar terms to ss 12GH(1) and (2) and apply to parties which are not body corporates.

Section 12GLD of the ASIC Act permits the court, on application by ASIC, to disqualify a party from managing corporations for an "appropriate" period, if the party has breached, or attempted to breach, certain provisions of Pt 2, Div 2 of the ASIC Act. In determining if disqualification is justified in the circumstances, ASIC will consider the party's conduct in managing any corporation, s 12GLD(2) of the ASIC Act. Section 12GLD of the ASIC Act closely mirrors s 248 of the ACL.

Fines

Section 12GC of the ASIC Act allows for fines to be enforced or recovered (where there has been failure to pay a fine). An order may be made declaring that the fine be enforced as a judgment debt. Failure to pay could result in imprisonment, s 12GC(5) of the ASIC Act. However, this section will not apply if the defendant provides security for the fine, s 12GC(2) of the ASIC Act. Any enforcement order will cease when either the fine is paid or the order is fully complied with, s 12GC(4) of the ASIC Act.

Injunctions

Section 12GD of the ASIC Act permits the court to grant injunctions for conduct which constitutes a breach. This includes relying on an unfair contract term, s 12GD(9) of the ASIC Act, or conduct which aids or abets a breach. Traditionally, an injunction is an equitable remedy. An injunction may:

- restrain a party from engaging in conduct
- restrain specific conduct only – **Qualifying injunction**
- restrain an apprehended or threatened breach of the ASIC Act – ***Quia timet* injunction,** ss 12GD(5) and (6) of the ASIC Act
- restrain a party, pending determination of an injunction – **Interim or interlocutory injunction,** s 12GD(3) of the ASIC Act, which largely mirrors s 234(1) of the ACL: *ASIC v Mayfair Wealth Partners Pty Ltd* [2020] FCA 494

- compel a party to act – **Mandatory injunction**, s 12GD(6) of the ASIC Act, or
- apply to both parties – **Cross-injunctions**.

Under s 12GD of the ASIC Act, the court can frame an injunction as essentially an order for specific performance of a contract. However, the terms of the injunction must be specific, and reasonably capable of being obeyed.

An applicant for an interlocutory injunction must show that there is (1) a serious question to be tried and (2) a balance of convenience in favour of granting an interlocutory order (2-limb test). Factors such as the harm caused to any one party and the public interest, will be relevant in assessing the balance of convenience. An applicant for an interlocutory injunction, other than ASIC or a Minister, must provide an undertaking as to damages, ss 12GD(7) and (8) of the ASIC Act.

Injunctions are, by their nature, oppressive, and courts traditionally proceed cautiously in exercising their discretion to grant an injunction: *ASIC v Burton-Clay* [2003] FCA 111. The fundamental question for the court is whether an injunction is appropriate in the circumstances, or whether the plaintiff could be adequately compensated by, for example, damages. An injunction is binding until varied or set aside.

Freezing assets

Section 12GN of the ASIC Act permits the court to freeze assets; that is, to essentially preserve assets by prohibiting a defendant to transfer any of their property in certain circumstances. Section 12GN of the ASIC Act closely mirrors s 137F of the Competition and Consumer Act.

Section 12GN(2) of the ASIC Act sets out the orders which the court can make. Before freezing a defendant's assets, the court must be satisfied that it is necessary or desirable to do so in order to preserve funds or property for potential future payment in fines, damages or compensation, s 12GN(1)(e). An order under s 12GN of the ASIC Act may prohibit a debtor from paying the defendant any outstanding debt, s 12GN(2)(a). Section 12GN of the ASIC Act has effect subject to the *Bankruptcy Act 1966 (Cth)*, s 12GN(7).

Damages

Section 12GF of the ASIC Act allows a plaintiff to recover damages for loss, as a result of unconscionable conduct which constitutes a breach. Section 12GF of the ASIC Act largely mirrors s 236 of the ACL and is drafted in broad terms. The provision is purely compensatory and does not contain any punitive element. An action seeking damages must be commenced within 6 years of the offending conduct, s 12GF(2) of the ASIC Act. However, limitation issues may arise where the effects of the offending conduct are seen over time, for example a gradual but ongoing loss of profits, or where the offending conduct has been concealed (for example, by fraud).

There must be actual **loss**: *Wardley Australia Ltd & Anor v The State of Western Australia* [1992] HCA 55, and only the person who suffers the loss can seek to recover it. Hence, the right cannot be assigned.

There must be a **causal connection** between the offending conduct and the loss suffered: *Brown & Anor v Jam Factory Pty Ltd & Anor* [1981] FCA 35. One test of causation is the "but for" test i.e. put simply, but for the defendant's breach, the plaintiff's loss would not have occurred: *Permanent Custodians Limited v Hoey* [2009] NSWSC 1073. However, the chain of causation may be broken by the acts of a third party. When it comes to **remoteness**, loss will be recoverable if it was reasonably foreseeable.

Interest on damages (from contravention to the date of judgment) may be awarded. The court must assess the quantum of damages as best it can, applying common sense. Sections 12GF(1A) and (1B) of the ASIC Act may **limit** the amount of damages which can be recovered in certain circumstances. This can include the application of professional standards law, under s 12GNA of the ASIC Act, if a professional standards law of a State or Territory applies to limit occupational liability in certain professions. Section 12GNA of the ASIC Act closely mirrors s 137 of the Competition and Consumer Act. Likewise, a plaintiff's failure to take reasonable care (**contributory negligence**) and mitigate their loss may also reduce the amount of damages payable, s 12GF(1B) of the ASIC Act. The measure of damages should restore the plaintiff to the position they would have been in had the offending conduct not occurred: *Gates v City Mutual Life Assurance Society Ltd* [1986] HCA 3.

Under s 12GG of the ASIC Act, a plaintiff for damages may be at an advantage if the defendant has already been found guilty of a breach of Pt 2, Div 2 of the ASIC Act in other proceedings, and that finding is supported by evidence, being a copy of the judgment. Hence, findings of fact in those earlier proceedings may be used in later proceedings.

Non-punitive orders

Section 12GLA of the ASIC Act permits a court to make non-punitive orders. The purpose of such orders is not to punish, but rather to deter breaches of the ASIC Act and to foster change. Section 12GLA of the ASIC Act closely mirrors s 246 of the ACL.

Examples of non-punitive orders include:

- Community service – Such as a community awareness program: *ACCC v Virgin Mobile Australia Pty Ltd (No 2)* [2002] FCA 1548
- Probation to prevent the offending conduct – Such as establishing a compliance or training program to change the corporate culture: *ASIC v Superannuation Warehouse Australia Pty Ltd* [2015] FCA 1167, or
- Corrective advertising – Which may deter from future breaches due to the fact that the offending conduct is made public: *ACCC v Wizard Mortgage Corporation Ltd* [2002] FCA 1317. However, any delay in ordering corrective advertising may have a punitive effect, in highlighting the defendant's breach (*ACCC v Bio Enviro Plan Pty Ltd* [2003] FCA 1219), or may simply be ineffective, due to the passage of time: *Medical Benefits Fund of Australia Ltd v Cassidy* [2003] FCAFC 289.

Adverse publicity orders

Section 12GLB of the ASIC Act gives the court power, on application by ASIC, to make an adverse publicity order in relation to a party who has been ordered to pay a pecuniary penalty or who is otherwise guilty of breaching the ASIC Act. An adverse publicity order requires the offending party to essentially "advertise" their offence. Hence, the order is punitive in nature and is aimed at deterring future contraventions of the ASIC Act and encouraging compliance. Section 12GLB of the ASIC Act closely mirrors s 247 of the ACL.

Public warning notices

Section 12GLC of the ASIC Act permits ASIC to issue public warning notices, essentially warning about a party's conduct which breaches, or may breach, provisions of Pt 2, Div 2 of the ASIC Act. Section 12GLC of the ASIC Act closely mirrors s 223 of the ACL. Under ss 12GLC(1)(a) – (c), ASIC may issue a notice where:

- there are reasonable grounds to suspect that certain conduct may breach the ASIC Act
- a party has suffered, or is likely to suffer, detriment as a result, and
- it is in the public interest to issue the notice.

Section 12GLC(2) of the ASIC Act refers to the situation where a party has failed to respond to a substantiation notice, and it is in the public interest to issue a warning notice.

Orders to compensate

If proceedings are already on foot for breach of Pt 2, Div 2 of the ASIC Act, s 12GM of the ASIC Act permits the court to make a range of orders to compensate parties for loss, whether already incurred or anticipated, s 12GM(2) of the ASIC Act. For anticipated loss there must be a real possibility or expectation of loss: *State of Western Australia v Wardley Australia Limited* (1991) 30 FCR 245. Hence, s 12GM is a wide "catch all" provision where an order, such as an injunction, may not suffice.

Section 12GM(7) of the ASIC Act provides a non-exhaustive list of the types of orders which a court can make. However, the court's power to grant relief under s 12GM is discretionary and orders under s 12GM may be made in addition to, or as alternatives to, any of the other orders as listed in sections 12GA – 12GO of the ASIC Act.

An application under s 12GM of the ASIC Act must be made within 6 years of the offending conduct, s 12GM(5) of the ASIC Act. Section 12GM allows the court to grant relief to an individual applicant only and not between parties (i.e. where each party may be liable for some aspect of the loss). Hence, there are some limitations to the provision.

Non-party consumers

Non-party consumers are those parties who are not privy to the contract, which is the subject of the unconscionable conduct, but who may be impacted by that conduct i.e. akin to third parties.

Sections 12GNB and 12GNC of the ASIC Act permit ASIC to apply to the court for orders to redress any loss or damage suffered by non-party consumers due to breach of the unconscionable conduct or consumer protection provisions of the ASIC Act or who are disadvantaged by a term in a consumer contract. Section 12GNB of the ASIC Act closely mirrors s 239 of the ACL.

Orders which the court can make include, but are not confined to, those orders as listed in s 12GNC of the ASIC Act. An application by ASIC under s 12GNB must be made within 6 years of the offending conduct, s 12GNB(5). The court is not obliged to determine which parties are relevant non-party consumers, s 12GNB(8)(a) of the ASIC Act.

Section 12GNB of the ASIC Act is subject to s 12GNA, which may limit the liability of a party for misleading or deceptive conduct if a professional standards law of a State or Territory applies, s 12GNB(10) of the ASIC Act.

Defences

Section 12GI(1) of the ASIC Act provides a number of statutory defences against prosecution. Provided that the defendant took reasonable precautions and exercised due diligence to avoid the breach, these defences include:

- reasonable mistake,
- reasonable reliance on information provided by another party,
- default of another party,
- an accident, or
- some other cause beyond the defendant's control.

A defendant bears the **onus of proof** for defences and the standard of proof is on the balance of probabilities. The defences are not mutually exclusive, meaning a defendant can rely on more than one defence.

"Reasonableness", in the context of a mistake, or reliance on information, is an objective test. "Reasonable mistake" generally refers to a one-off incident and not a systematic or ongoing pattern of behaviour. An individual may be more likely to succeed in pleading a defence of reasonable mistake than a corporation: *ACCC v Anglo Estates Pty Ltd* [2005] FCA 20. For a defence of reasonable reliance, or default by another party, to succeed, there must be an attempt to identify the "other party", s 12GI(3) of the ASIC Act.

Section 12GI(4) of the ASIC Act sets out the "publisher's defence" which protects a publisher in the ordinary course of business where the publisher did not know, and had no reason to suspect, that a publication (such as an advertisement) would be in breach of the provisions relating to consumer protection or deferred sales for add-on insurance products: *Cassidy v NRMA Health Pty Ltd* [2002] FCA 1228. Section 12GI(5) of the ASIC Act sets out the defence of acting honestly and reasonably, for parties who are not body corporates. However, whether this defence will apply is at the discretion of the court.

Jurisdiction

Section 12GJ(1) of the ASIC Act confers **jurisdiction** on the Federal Court, State Courts vested with federal jurisdiction, or Territory Courts pursuant to the Constitution, in matters arising under Pt 2, Div 2 of the ASIC Act. Sections 12GK and 12GL of the ASIC Act allow matters to be transferred between Federal, State and Territory courts.

Under s 12GO of the ASIC Act, **ASIC may intervene** in a proceeding under Pt 2, Div 2 of the ASIC Act, provided that ASIC has leave of the court. The result is that ASIC becomes a party to the proceeding, with all the inherent rights, duties and liabilities. The court may grant leave if the application raises public interest and ASIC expresses a legitimate concern as to the outcome: *Auskay International Manufacturing & Trade Pty Ltd v Qantas Airways Ltd* [2010] FCA 521.

Under s 12GBCH of the ASIC Act, any civil proceedings will be stayed if **related criminal proceedings** have already been commenced

Other provisions

Additional enforcement and remedy principles, which do not naturally fall under any of the preceding headings, are:

- Section 12GBCG – Contains the **rule against double jeopardy**
- Section 12GCA(2)(b) – **Plaintiff's compensation takes priority.** Preference must be given to compensate parties who suffer loss as a result of a breach. This is relevant where a defendant's capacity to pay a fine, or other order, may subsequently impact on their ability to compensate the plaintiff. In this case, the plaintiff's compensation takes priority. Section 12GCA(2)(b) of the ASIC Act closely mirrors s 227 of the ACL.
- Section 12GND – **Unfair contract terms**. This provision permits the court to declare a term in a small business contract, or a consumer contract, to be unfair if it meets the tests of unfairness in s 12BG of the ASIC Act, provided that the contract is a standard form contract for financial services. This provision now extends to third party beneficiaries of insurance contracts, within the meaning of the *Insurance Contracts Act 1984 (Cth)*. In determining whether to apply to the court, ASIC may make such investigations into the terms of the relevant contract, as it thinks fit, ss 13(7) and (8) of the ASIC Act.

¶6-070 ASIC's Role in Proportionate Liability for Misleading and Deceptive Conduct

Sections 12GP – 12GW of the ASIC Act deal with proportionate liability in misleading and deceptive conduct. These provisions apply to misleading and deceptive conduct only, namely s 12DA of the ASIC Act. This was confirmed by the High Court in *Selig v Wealthsure Pty Ltd* (2015) 255 CLR 661.

Loss caused by more than one party

Proportionate liability applies where loss or damage has been caused by the conduct of two or more defendants, whereby the doctrine limits a defendant's liability to only that specific portion of the damage for which the defendant is responsible. Hence, a plaintiff can recover from a particular defendant only the portion of the loss for which that particular defendant is responsible.

Section 12GP of the ASIC Act defines the defendants as **concurrent wrongdoers**. A "concurrent wrongdoer" is a party whose acts or omissions, contributed to the damage or loss which is the subject of the claim. It is irrelevant that a concurrent wrongdoer is insolvent, being wound up, has ceased to exist or has died, s 12GP(5) of the ASIC Act.

Section 12GR of the ASIC Act sets out the provision for proportionate liability. A concurrent wrongdoer's liability for an apportionable claim is limited to the portion of damage or loss which relates to their wrongdoing. It is important to note that any contributory negligence, on the part of the plaintiff, is also considered, s 12GR(3)(a) of the ASIC Act.

Apportionable claims

Under s 12GP of the ASIC Act, proportionate liability applies only to apportionable claims – that is, a claim made under s 12GF of the ASIC Act, for loss or damage caused by misleading or deceptive conduct in breach of s 12DA of the ASIC Act. Generally, once a court has apportioned the shares of damages between the defendant(s), this apportionment cannot subsequently be altered.

Proportionate liability as a defence

Proportionate liability can be used as a defence in order to limit a defendant's liability to their portion of the damage. However, under s 12GQ of the ASIC Act, certain concurrent wrongdoers are **excluded** from the benefits of apportionment. This applies to concurrent wrongdoers who acted with intent or who fraudulently caused the loss or damage which is the subject of the claim.

Other provisions

The remaining substantive provisions of the ASIC Act for regulating and governing proportionate liability are:

- Section 12GS – A defendant must **notify the plaintiff** in writing of a party who they suspect to be a concurrent wrongdoer, as soon as practicable; otherwise, the defendant may be liable for all the costs in the proceedings.
- Section 12GT – **Other wrongdoers**. A defendant is not required to contribute to any damages or contribution imposed on another wrongdoer, or to indemnify any such wrongdoer.
- Section 12GU – **Subsequent actions**. A plaintiff can bring an action against a concurrent wrongdoer even if the plaintiff previously brought an action against *another* concurrent wrongdoer for the *same* damage or loss.
- Section 12GV – **Joining non-parties**. Permits the court to join one or more parties as defendants in proceedings involving an apportionable claim, unless a party was already a defendant to any previous proceedings for the same apportionable claim.
- Section 12GW – A party (A) can be held **vicariously liable** for a portion of an apportionable claim, for which another party (B) is liable, s 12GW(a). In a similar way, a party (X) can be held **severally liable** with another party (Y) for that proportion of an apportionable claim for which Y is liable.

¶6-080 ASIC's Role in Issuing Infringement Notices

Sections 12GX – 12GXH of the ASIC Act permit ASIC to issue infringement notices for suspected contraventions of civil pecuniary penalty provisions of the ASIC Act. Infringement notices supplement existing criminal sanctions and civil penalties.

An infringement notice is not the imposition of a financial penalty by ASIC; rather, it is the first step in that process. Receiving an infringement notice permits a defendant to anticipate an application to the courts by ASIC for the imposition of a criminal sanction or civil penalty. Hence, the infringement notice regime allows ASIC to take action against less serious breaches of, for example, unfair practices, more efficiently than through the courts. ASIC Information Sheet – INFO 139: *Australian Consumer Law infringement notices: Your rights* – sets out further guidance on infringement notices.

The infringement notice regime was replaced in full by the *Treasury Laws Amendment (Strengthening Corporate and Financial Sector Penalties) Act 2019 (Cth)*. The substantive provisions are:

Timing

Under s 12GX of the ASIC Act, an infringement notice must be given within 12 months of the offending conduct, s 12GX(2) of the ASIC Act.

Provisions subject to an infringement notice

Section 12GXA of the ASIC Act details the provisions subject to an infringement notice. This includes the unconscionable conduct provisions (ss 12CA – 12CC of the ASIC Act) and a large portion of the consumer protection provisions, as well as the substantiation notice provisions (ss 12GY – 12GYC of the ASIC Act).

Infringement notice

Section 12GXB of the ASIC Act outlines the matters to be included in an infringement notice. These matters include a number of formal and administrative requirements.

Payment of infringement notices

Section 12GXC(1) of the ASIC Act specifies the **payment period** as 28 days from the date of receipt of the notice. ASIC may choose to extend this period under s 12GXD(2) of the ASIC Act. Section 12GXE of the ASIC Act allows a defendant to apply to ASIC to pay the notice by instalments. Section 12GXG of the ASIC Act confirms the **effect of payment** of the infringement notice – that is, the defendant's liability is discharged, and they cannot be prosecuted or subject to an order.

Non-issue and withdrawal of infringement notice

Under s 12GXH of the ASIC Act, ASIC may choose **not to issue** an infringement notice, s 12GXH(a). Such a decision is entirely at ASIC's **discretion**.

Section 12GXF of the ASIC Act permits a defendant to apply to ASIC to **withdraw** an infringement notice. In deciding whether to withdraw a notice, ASIC may take into account the defendant's past behaviour, s 12GXF(4) of the ASIC Act. If ASIC withdraws the notice following payment of the penalty by the defendant, ASIC must subsequently refund the defendant, s 12GXF(7) of the ASIC Act.

A decision not to issue, or to withdraw, an infringement notice, does not affect a party's liability for any breach of the ASIC Act, s 12GXH(b) of the ASIC Act. Such a breach may simply be dealt with via another enforcement provision. The court also has full discretion to determine the penalty amount applicable to an infringement notice, s 12GXH(d) of the ASIC Act.

¶6-090 ASIC's Role in Issuing Substantiation Notices

Sections 12GY – 12GYC of the ASIC Act permit ASIC to issue substantiation notices relating to consumer protection in certain circumstances.

A substantiation notice corroborates and **supports any representations** or statements made by a party, such as a financial service provider, for the services they promote. This may be achieved by using the substantiation notice to request further supporting documents of the party under investigation. Hence, the power provides ASIC with a **preliminary investigative tool** if ASIC suspects that a representation may be in breach of the ASIC Act because it is false, misleading or deceptive. Failure to comply with a substantiation notice may only serve to corroborate or support ASIC's suspicions and will likely lead to further enforcement action.

ASIC Information Sheet – INFO 140: *Australian Consumer Law substantiation notices: Your rights* – sets out further guidance on substantiation notices.

The substantive provisions are:

Issuing a substantiation notice

Section 12GY of the ASIC Act permits ASIC to issue a substantiation notice for a party to produce certain documents to support their claims, s 12GY(2) of the ASIC Act. The substantiation notice must include certain information, s 12GY(4) of the ASIC Act. The information sought by ASIC must be relevant, s 12GY(3), and a party must not give ASIC any false or misleading information in response to a substantiation notice, s 12GYC of the ASIC Act.

Certain parties, such as prescribed information providers, and those who publish information in a commercial context, are exempt from substantiation notices, s 12GY(6) of the ASIC Act.

Complying with a substantiation notice

Under s 12GYB of the ASIC Act, a party who has received a substantiation notice must comply with it within the "**substantiation notice compliance period**", defined as 21 days, unless that period is extended under s 12GYA of the ASIC Act, which permits a party to apply for an extension.

However, under s 12GYB(3) of the ASIC Act, a party may refuse to provide certain information on the grounds that it may incriminate them or expose them to a penalty.

¶6-100 ASIC's Role in Administering Miscellaneous Provisions of the ASIC Act

Sections 12HA – 12HD of the ASIC Act contain a number of miscellaneous provisions which support the operation of Pt 2, Div 2 of the ASIC Act. These miscellaneous provisions can be summarised as:

Powers of investigation and information-gathering

Section 12HA of the ASIC Act, states that any powers conferred on ASIC by Pt 2, Div 2 of the ASIC Act, and any restrictions on those powers, are in addition to ASIC's general **powers of investigation and information-gathering** under Pt 3 of the ASIC Act. Hence, ASIC may utilise any of its powers conferred by both Pts 2 and 3 of the ASIC Act in investigations.

Disclosure of documents

Section 12HB of the ASIC Act regulates the disclosure of documents by ASIC in certain proceedings under Pt 2, Div 2 of the ASIC Act. ASIC must, upon payment of any prescribed fee, provide a party to the proceedings with copies of any documents obtained by ASIC relating to, or tending to establish, the party's case, s 12HB(1) of the ASIC Act. If ASIC fails to comply with such a request, the party may apply to the court, and the court must make the order unless it would be inappropriate for the court to do so, because disclosure may prejudice a party, or for any other reason: ss 12HB(2) and (3) of the ASIC Act. When it comes to disclosure, and in exercising its discretion, the court is likely to exercise caution where documents are protected by legal professional privilege: *ACCC v Trading Post Australia Pty Ltd* [2008] FCA 1298.

Jurisdiction

Section 12HC of the ASIC Act confers exclusive jurisdiction on the Federal Court to hear prosecutions for offences against Pt 2, Div 2 of the ASIC Act, or offences against Pt 3 of the Act, as it applies to investigations of contraventions of Pt 2, Div 2 of the Act.

Section 12HD of the ASIC Act confers jurisdiction on the Federal Court to make declarations and orders (including for example, prohibition) about the operation or effect of certain provisions of Pt 2, Div 2 and Pt 3 of the ASIC Act, as it applies to investigations of contraventions of Pt 2, Div 2. It should be noted that this is a specific head of jurisdiction, additional to the general jurisdiction of the Federal Court, as conferred by the *Federal Court of Australia Act 1976 (Cth)*. Proceedings seeking any such declaration or order may be instituted by a "person". Such "person" may include the Minister who can also intervene in proceedings already on foot. Whether or not a declaration should be made is in the court's discretion: *Emirates v ACCC* [2009] FCA 312.

Chapter 7

ASIC'S ROLE IN INVESTIGATIONS AND INFORMATION-GATHERING

ASIC has an over-arching role to investigate any breaches, or suspected breaches, of the ASIC Act, Corporations Act or other relevant State or Territory laws.

It is important to note that an investigation is not a judicial proceeding; rather, it is a process by which ASIC gathers further information on the legislative breach or suspected legislative breach. This information-gathering process is achieved through the examinations of persons and company documents (referred to as books). The outcome of an ASIC investigation may be the commencement of an ASIC hearing, with a view to prosecution or the imposition of a penalty on the party in breach.

This chapter discusses ASIC's role in investigations, information-gathering, hearings and the imposition of any penalties.

¶7-000 ASIC's Role in Investigations

Sections 13 – 15 of the ASIC Act outline the types of investigations in which ASIC can engage. Sections 16 – 18 of the ASIC Act outline the types of **reports** which ASIC must prepare, following an investigation.

General powers of investigation

Section 13 of the ASIC Act contains ASIC's general powers of investigation. These powers **exclude** s 12A of the ASIC Act (which relates to ASIC's other functions and powers). Under s 13 of the ASIC Act, there is no need for a formal, written, commencement of an investigation.

The circumstances which empower ASIC to conduct an investigation under s 13 of the ASIC Act, include:

ASIC suspects a breach of the legislation

Under s 13(1) of the ASIC Act, ASIC may suspect a breach of the ASIC Act, Corporations Act or a relevant State or Territory law relating to managed investment schemes or financial products. Section 13(1) of the ASIC Act confers ASIC with broad investigative power and extends to both anticipated civil and criminal proceedings: *ASIC v Plymin & Ors (No 2)* (2002) 20 ACLC 1.

However, ASIC must have a "reason to suspect" breach of the legislation, meaning both an honest suspicion (beyond mere speculation) and a just cause for that suspicion: *NCSC v Sim (No 2)* (1986) 11 ACLR 171. Hence, suspicion on the part of ASIC is a necessary prerequisite to a s 13 investigation. In holding a suspicion, there is no need for ASIC to nominate a particular suspected defendant or individual. If, however, ASIC *has* a particular party in mind, there is likewise no obligation on ASIC to notify that party about the conduct of the investigation: *Karounos & Anor v CAC & Ors* (1989) 7 ACLC 567.

Under s 13 of the ASIC Act, ASIC also has the power to expand the scope of an investigation beyond the initial suspected breach. This may result in ASIC uncovering additional breaches which were not originally contemplated: *ASC v Graco* (1991) 9 ACLC 828.

ASIC suspects that unacceptable circumstances have occurred

Under s 13(2) of the ASIC Act, ASIC may suspect that unacceptable circumstances have occurred within the meaning of Pt 6.10, Div 2, Subdiv B of the Corporations Act (relating to the Takeovers Panel). This may result in ASIC applying to the Takeovers Panel under s 657 of the Corporations Act, for a declaration in relation to unacceptable circumstances. "Unacceptable circumstances" may arise where Company A acquires a substantial interest in Company B, as a result of a proposed takeover, which may subsequently impact on market competition or result in a monopoly.

ASIC suspects that a registered liquidator has not faithfully performed their duties

Under s 13(3) of the ASIC Act, ASIC may suspect that a registered liquidator has not faithfully performed their duties, including their fiduciary duties (which are not codified in the ASIC Act or the Corporations Act). It is for this reason that specific provision has been made in s 13(3) of the ASIC Act to empower ASIC to investigate liquidators' conduct generally. ASIC also has the power, under Sch 2 of the Corporations Act, to inquire into the performance of liquidators' duties.

ASIC suspects breach of the unconscionable conduct and consumer protection provisions

Under s 13(6) of the ASIC Act, ASIC may suspect a breach of the provisions of Pt 2, Div 2 of the ASIC Act (which govern unconscionable conduct and consumer protection in relation to financial services).

ASIC suspects that unfair contract terms exist

Under s 13(7) of the ASIC Act, ASIC may conduct an investigation into the terms of a small business or consumer contract, for the purpose of assessing if the terms may be unfair. If so, ASIC may then proceed to make an application to the court under s 12GND of the ASIC Act (which deals with declarations by the court).

Investigations directed by the Minister

Section 14 of the ASIC Act allows for ASIC investigations as directed by the Minister, if it is in the public interest, s 14(1) of the ASIC Act. A Minister's direction to ASIC must be in writing, and ASIC must comply with the direction, s 14(3) of the ASIC Act, although ASIC may still delegate its powers and functions under s 14(4) of the ASIC Act.

The matter for investigation must be one which falls within those matters, as listed under s 14(2)(b) of the ASIC Act. These matters relate to:

- the affairs of a body corporate
- financial products and markets – such as a securities market
- clearing and settlement facilities – such as ASX Settlement
- derivative trade repositories – which are regulated under Pt 7.5A of the Corporations Act.

Investigation following receipt of a liquidator report

Section 15 of the ASIC Act permits ASIC to conduct an investigation following receipt of a liquidator or receiver report or return, lodged pursuant to ss 422, 422A, 422B or 533 of the Corporations Act. Liquidator or receiver reports may indicate that a company officer is guilty of negligence or breach of duty, such as misappropriation of funds, or may indicate that the company is unable to pay its debts. Under the Corporations Act, liquidators and receivers are obliged to assist ASIC in any investigations, including furnishing any required documents. A liquidator, or receiver, can also lodge other reports with ASIC in order to bring any other matter to ASIC's attention as they see fit.

Interim investigation report

Section 16 of the ASIC Act obliges ASIC to prepare an interim investigation report if ASIC forms the opinion that:

- a serious breach of the legislation has occurred,
- an interim report may assist in protecting, preserving or recovering property, or

- there is an urgent need for the ASIC Act and/or the Corporations Act to be amended.

An "opinion" will essentially be formed by officers of ASIC but must be sufficiently attributable to ASIC itself. ASIC must also prepare an interim report if directed by the Minister to do so, s 16(2) of the ASIC Act. The report must set out matters relating to the investigation, as ASIC thinks fit, or as directed by the Minister, s 16(3) of the ASIC Act. This may include ASIC's findings and evidence to date.

Final investigation report

Section 17 of the ASIC Act covers the preparation by ASIC of a final investigation report at the end of an investigation under ss 13 – 15 of the ASIC Act. ASIC retains a discretion to prepare a final report for investigation under ss 13 or 15 of the ASIC Act, unless directed by the Minister to do so, s 17(1) of the ASIC Act. The final report must set out ASIC's findings, supported by evidence of any other matters which ASIC sees fit to include, or as directed by the Minister, s 17(3) of the ASIC Act.

Section 18 of the ASIC Act deals with **distribution of the report**. Section 18(1) of the ASIC Act requires that a copy of the final report be provided to the Minister, who can cause the whole report, or a part of the report, to be published, s 18(4) of the ASIC Act. If the report relates to a serious breach of the law, ASIC may also provide a copy to the Australian Federal Police, Director of Public Prosecutions, or a prescribed agency such as APRA or the Australian Taxation Office, s 18(2) of the ASIC Act and ASIC Regulation 3.

¶7-010 ASIC's Role in Examination of Persons

The next step in ASIC's investigatory role is to examine persons, whom ASIC believe, can assist in an investigation. An examination, like an investigation of which it forms part, is not a judicial proceeding. Examinations are one of the most "delicate" of ASIC roles, due to the sensitive nature of questioning parties, and there are several provisions, under ss 19 – 27 of the ASIC Act, governing its conduct. These provisions are detailed below.

Notice of examination

Under s 19 of the ASIC Act, ASIC must issue a notice for attendance at an examination. This can be issued to a party whom ASIC believes, on reasonable grounds, can provide information or assist in an ASIC investigation, s 19(1) of the ASIC Act. The notice must be in writing in the prescribed form, s 19(2) of the ASIC Act. "Prescribed form" must include a statement as to the effect of s 23(1) (right to legal representation at an examination) and s 68 (privilege against self-incrimination) of the ASIC Act. The notice must also state the "general nature of the matter", s 19(3) of the ASIC Act: *Kennedy v ASIC* (2005) 23 ACLC 358. Listing the provisions which are in breach (if applicable and appropriate) may assist in describing the "general nature of the matter": *Australian Securities Commission v Avram* (1997) 15 ACLC 70. The notice requires a party to attend an examination under oath, pursuant to s 19(2)(b) of the ASIC Act.

ASIC's s 19 examination powers may relate to anticipated proceedings under either the ASIC Act or the Corporations Act: *ASIC v Plymin & Ors (No 2)* (2002) 20 ACLC 1. However, ASIC's examination powers do not necessarily cease once proceedings commence: *ASIC v Elm Financial Services* (2004) 22 ACLC 1. Although, under s 127 of the ASIC Act, ASIC has confidentiality obligations to protect information disclosed to it, ASIC may provide a s 19 transcript of examination for use in proceedings, unless the transcript is protected by the privilege against self-incrimination under s 68 of the ASIC Act: *R v Jacobson (Ruling No 4)* (2014) 32 ACLC. Because there is an expectation that the transcript will be used in proceedings, it would also be difficult to claim procedural unfairness or prejudice to the defendant as a result of its use.

Obligations on examinee

Under s 21 of the ASIC Act, the obligations on the party being examined (the examinee) include the requirement to take an oath or affirmation, s 21(1) of the ASIC Act, the purpose of which is to ensure that the examinee answers truthfully, s 21(2) of the ASIC Act. Failure of an examinee to comply with s 21(1) is an offence of strict liability, s 21(1A) of the ASIC Act.

Examination to take place in private

Section 22 of the ASIC Act mandates that an examination take place in private, and the party conducting the examination (the inspector) may give directions, under s 22(1) of the ASIC Act, as to who should be present at the examination. This discretionary power is vested in the inspector in their own capacity and means that an examinee's lawyer can be excluded from the examination, but only if the inspector, in good faith, reasonably believes that such exclusion is necessary: *ASC v Bell* (1991) 9 ACLC 1.

Hence, the discretionary power in s 22(1) of the ASIC Act can essentially encroach on s 23(1) of the ASIC Act (which permits an examinee's lawyer to attend), but only where the inspector believes that encroachment is necessary for proper conduct of the examination which is the overriding purpose. Also, despite the discretion, an inspector must still act with **procedural fairness** in determining who can attend an examination: *Collard v ASIC (No 3)* [2008] FCA 1681. ASIC may make **non-disclosure** orders in relation to private examinations; however such orders operate only while the investigation is on foot "to protect the integrity and efficacy" of the process: *Gangemi & Liedermoy v ASIC* (2003) 21 ACLC 1. Failure to comply with s 22(1) of the ASIC Act is an offence of strict liability, s 22(3) of the ASIC Act.

Examinee's lawyer may attend examination

Under s 23 of the ASIC Act, a lawyer may attend an examination, although this may not necessarily be the examinee's lawyer of choice: *Stockbridge v Ogilvie* (1993) 11 ACLC 645. Hence, s 23(1) of the ASIC Act essentially ensures a basic right to **legal representation**. Under s 23(1) of the ASIC Act, the lawyer may address the inspector and question the examinee, unless the inspector believes that the lawyer is trying to obstruct or sabotage the examination, s 23(2) of the ASIC Act. ASIC may have the power to exclude a *particular* lawyer from an examination, notwithstanding that lawyer's express right to be present: *ASC v Bell* (1991) 9 ACLC 1,606.

Record of examination

Sections 24 – 27 of the ASIC Act govern the provision of a record of the examination, s 24(1) of the ASIC Act. If the record is in writing, the inspector may require the examinee to sign it: s 24(2)(a) of the ASIC Act. The record then becomes *prima facie* evidence of the statements therein. However, an examinee may not be obliged to sign a record of examination if to do so results in self-incrimination: *Green v Purdon & Anor* (1987) 5 ACLC 407. The examinee is entitled to a copy of the record, on written request and without charge, but subject to any conditions as imposed by the inspector, s 24(2)(b) of the ASIC Act. Such conditions may relate to maintaining confidentiality of all, or part, of the record.

Disclosure of record of examination

Section 25 of the ASIC Act permits ASIC to disclose written records of its examination to other parties. Such disclosure is voluntary (controlled by ASIC) and not in response to a subpoena (disclosure controlled by the court): *Maronis Holdings Ltd & Ors v Nippon Credit Australia Ltd & Ors* (2000) 18 ACLC 609. Disclosure may be to a party's lawyer, where the lawyer is carrying on, or contemplating, proceedings to which the examination relates, s 25(1) of the ASIC Act. Hence the intention is for the examination to assist in litigation: *Gray v ASIC* (2002) 20 ACLC 1.

ASIC's confidentiality obligations under s 127 of the ASIC Act do not apply under s 25. In any case, disclosure pursuant to s 25(1) of the ASIC Act is taken to be authorised disclosure under s 127(3): *Johns v ASC* (1993) 11 ACLC 1. However, disclosure under s 25(1) of the ASIC Act is at ASIC's discretion and may be refused upon a ground of, for example, anticipated prejudice to a continuing investigation. Section 25(2) of the ASIC Act protects the copyright of the record of examination, breach of which is an offence of strict liability, s 25(2A) of the ASIC Act.

ASIC Regulatory Guide – RG 103 *Confidentiality and release of information* – sets out further guidance on the operation of s 25 of the ASIC Act. Refer also to our ***NOTE*** below on the operation of s 127 of the ASIC Act which imposes confidentiality obligations on ASIC.

Section 26 of the ASIC Act obliges a party who receives a record of examination, under ss 24(2) or 25(3) of the ASIC Act, to comply with the **conditions** as stipulated, s 26(1) of the ASIC Act. Breach of s 26(1) of the ASIC Act is an offence of strict liability, s 26(2) of the ASIC Act.

Section 27 of the ASIC Act states that an examination **record must accompany a report** from ASIC (being a final investigation report, produced by ASIC under s 17 of the ASIC Act), s 27(1) of the ASIC Act. This is also required if ASIC believes that a statement made at an examination is relevant to any other investigation, s 27(2) of the ASIC Act.

A note on ASIC's role in protecting confidential information – Section 127 of the ASIC Act

Under s 127 of the ASIC Act, ASIC is obliged to protect the confidentiality of information provided to it for the performance of its role, except for "excluded provisions" or "protected information", s 127(1) of the ASIC Act. However, producing documents in response to a court order or subpoena is unlikely to breach s 127: *ASC v Zarro & Ors (No 2)* (1992) 10 ACLC 553.

Section 127 of the ASIC Act lists several **authorised disclosures** including information:

- in summary form – From which an individual cannot be identified, s 127(1A)
- required to be disclosed by legislation, s 127(2)
- made to the Minister for the purpose of advice, or to a body, s 127(2A)
- made to a Royal Commission, ss 127(2B) and (2C)
- obtained by ASIC during the exercise of its audit functions, ss 127(2D)–(2G). ASIC must give an auditor at least 7 days' notice of its intention to disclose "performance" information to the audit client, s 127(2F)
- made for the purposes of performing ASIC functions, s 127(3)
- for the purposes of the Asia Region Funds Passport, s 127(3AA)
- where disclosure is consented to, s 127(3A)
- made by an authorised party, s 127(4), or
- made to a financial body corporate, ss 127(4B) and (4C).

If an examination transcript is to be disclosed to a State or Territory government agency, under s 127(4)(b), ASIC must observe the **rules of natural justice**: *Johns v*

ASC (1993) 11 ACLC 1. This involves ensuring that the agency observes the transcript's confidentiality, and that the defendant is afforded an opportunity, if appropriate, to oppose transfer of their information to the agency. ASIC acknowledges that parties adversely affected by a decision to release information are entitled to natural justice. This may require ASIC to hear submissions from affected parties including any conditions which should be imposed on the recipient.

Further guidance:

- ASIC Regulatory Guide – RG 103 – *Confidentiality and release of information* – Sets out **ASIC policy on confidentiality**.
- ASIC Regulatory Guide – RG 260 – *Communicating findings from audit files to directors, audit committees or senior managers* – provides further guidance on disclosure within ASIC's audit functions.
- ASIC Regulatory Guide – RG 92: *Procedural fairness to third parties* – ASIC must take confidentiality into account in deciding whether to release information to third parties.

¶7-020 ASIC's Role in Inspection of Books

Sections 28 – 39C of the ASIC Act allow ASIC to issue notices for the inspection of company books relating to, for example, a company's affairs. These provisions are documented below.

Limitations on ASIC's power

Section 28 of the ASIC Act restricts ASIC's power to inspect books to certain cases only. These include:

- for the performance of ASIC functions,
- to ensure compliance with the ASIC Act and/or the Corporations Act,
- for a suspected breach of the ASIC Act and/or the Corporations Act, or
- for the purposes of investigation.

The power to ensure legislative compliance is broad and hence does not serve as a restriction in the strictest sense: *Financial Custodian Corporation of Victoria Pty Ltd & Ors v Taylor & Anor* (1991) 9 ACLC 1. A "suspected breach" requires an "actual apprehension" of breach and not just a mere wondering: *Queensland Bacon Pty Ltd v Rees* (1966) 115 CLR 266.

Similar restrictions apply in s 40 of the ASIC Act in the context of ASIC requesting disclosure of information.

Public interest immunity, a common law doctrine, may also provide a defence against producing a document, if it would be injurious to the public interest to disclose it: *Sankey v Whitlam* (1978) 142 CLR 1; See also *Zarro & Ors v ASC* (1992) 10 ACLC 831. A claim for public interest immunity must state why disclosure would be detrimental in the circumstances. However, this must be balanced against the public interest in administration of justice: *Conway v Rimmer* [1968] AC 910, and protecting the informer, in order to encourage future informers: *ASIC v P Dawson Nominees Pty Ltd* (2008) 26 ACLC 825. This willing cooperation of informers is particularly important from ASIC's perspective. It allows for timely and targeted investigations and may also inform ASIC of further breaches or misconduct beyond ASIC's initial contemplation. Public interest immunity cannot be waived by the Crown or any other party: *Air Canada v Secretary of State for Trade* [1983] 2 AC 394.

It should also be noted that parties providing information to ASIC are protected, as corporate whistleblowers, under Pt 9.4AAA of the Corporations Act. Hence, for disclosure to ASIC, the common law doctrine of public interest immunity should be applied consistently with Corporations Act, Pt 9.4AAA legislative policy.

Inspection of books

Under s 29 of the ASIC Act, ASIC can inspect books, required to be kept by a corporation, without charge. The books must be made available for inspection, s 29(2) of the ASIC Act. ASIC's authorisation under this section may be general or limited by reference to the books to be inspected, s 29(3) of the ASIC Act. The term "books" is broad and includes financial reports, records or a register.

Notices to produce books

An ASIC notice to product books must specify a place and time which is **reasonable** in all the circumstances. If reasonable, ASIC may require immediate production of the books, s 87 of the ASIC Act. The ASIC provisions, governing notices to produce books, are detailed below.

Section 30 of the ASIC Act outlines the notice requirements for books relating to **affairs of a body corporate or registered scheme**. This may include documents such as personal diaries of appointments: *ASC v Lord* (1992) 10 ACLC 50. The requirement that the books relate to company affairs is absolute and must be proved: *ASC v Lucas* (1992) 10 ACLC 888. Notice must be in writing and specify the time and place of production and the specific books to be produced, s 30(1) of the ASIC Act. It must also specify the "nature of the matter" so that, at a minimum, the recipient can assess if the notice is within power. A s 30 notice need not specify the legal basis on which it is given; however, failure to identify the source of ASIC's power in the notice may expose it to scrutiny: *ASC v Lucas* (1992) 10 ACLC 888. Section 30 of the ASIC Act does not permit ASIC to seize books: *Camilla Holdings Pty Ltd v International Task Pty Ltd (in liq) & Anor* (1987) 5 ACLC 972, and the power must be exercised cautiously.

Section 30A of the ASIC Act outlines the notice requirements for books relating to **audit**. The notice is issued to an auditor. However, the power can be exercised only if it meets the purpose tests as set out in s 30A(2) of the ASIC Act which relate to audit matters and audit investigations under various legislation. Under s 30A(3) of the ASIC Act, ASIC can request books relating to audit policies and procedures. An auditor must comply with a s 30A(1) notice, even if producing the books results in a breach of confidentiality to the audited body, s 30A(4) of the ASIC Act. This provision ensures that an auditor cannot be sued by an audited body for complying with an ASIC order. Under s 30A(5) of the ASIC Act, ASIC may extend the period for an auditor to produce the books.

Section 30B of the ASIC Act outlines the notice requirements for books relating to **liquidation affairs**. The notice is issued to a liquidator. However, the power can be exercised only if it meets the purpose tests as set out in s 30B(2) of the ASIC Act which relate to liquidation requirements, suspected breach of those requirements and investigations into liquidations. Under s 30B(4) of the ASIC Act, ASIC can request books relating to liquidation policies and procedures, external administrations and control of companies by liquidators. A liquidator must comply with a s 30B(1) notice, even if producing the books results in a breach of confidentiality to the liquidated company, s 30B(5) of the ASIC Act. This ensures that a liquidator cannot be sued by the company for complying with an ASIC order. Under s 30B(6) of the ASIC Act, ASIC may extend the period for a liquidator to produce the books.

Section 31 of the ASIC Act outlines the notice requirements for books relating to **financial products**. Under this section, ASIC may issue a notice to a financial adviser, investment adviser or operator of a financial market, amongst others, ss 31(1)(a) – (f) of the ASIC Act. Books to be produced include those dealing with the business affairs of a financial market, dealings (*Controlled Consultants Pty Ltd v Commissioner for Corporate Affairs* (1985) 3 ACLC 136), advice or audit reports, ss 31(1)(g) – (m) of the ASIC Act. Section 31(2) of the ASIC Act extends the provisions of s 31 of the Act to a trustee.

Section 32A of the ASIC Act outlines the notice requirements for books relating to **financial services**. The notice is issued to a financial service provider. "Financial service" includes providing a "financial product", as defined under s 12BAB of the ASIC Act. Notice must be in writing and specify the time and place of production. ASIC's s 32A examination powers do not necessarily cease if proceedings commence: *ASIC v Elm Financial Services* (2004) 22 ACLC 1.

Section 33 of the ASIC Act outlines the notice requirements for **documents in possession** of a party. The notice can be issued to a party not necessarily related to the corporation being investigated. Hence, s 33 of the ASIC Act serves as a "catch all" provision for parties who do not strictly fall into the ss 30 – 32A categories. A s 33 notice must be sufficiently clear, to identify what is required and ensure the books requested are within ASIC's power. Books to be produced can include those relating to audit, liquidation or the affairs of a body corporate or registered scheme, ss 33(1) – (3) of the ASIC Act.

"Possession" means a book is in a party's custody or under their control: *Green v FP Special Assets Ltd & Ors* (1991) 9 ACLC, implying that the party has the capacity to service the request; it is not concerned with property rights or legal entitlement of the books: *Integrated Financial Group v ASIC* (2004) 22 ACLC 987. Hence, a book can be produced even if a party's possession of it is unlawful. ASIC is not obliged to show a nexus between the books sought and the corporation being investigated: *ASC v Zarro & Ors* (1992) 10 ACLC 11. A party's obligation to respond to a s 33 notice takes priority over any obligations of confidentiality to a party who may be prejudiced by release of the books. Hence, confidentiality obligations or any undertaking of confidentiality, fail to provide a reasonable excuse for non-compliance with s 33: *ASC v Zarro & Ors* (1992) 10 ACLC 11. Likewise, legal professional privilege does not apply: *CAC of NSW v Yuill & Ors* (1991) 9 ACLC 843.

Authority to request books

Section 34 of the ASIC Act permits ASIC to provide a party with **authority** to request production of books. That authorisation may be general or limited to certain parties, books or information, ss 34(2)(a) – (c) of the ASIC Act. The practical effect of s 34 of the ASIC Act is that any reference to ASIC in ss 30 – 33 of the Act is taken to be a reference to the party so authorised.

Powers where books produced or not produced

Section 37 of the ASIC Act outlines powers to deal with **books which have been produced** in response to a notice or seized under a warrant. The party then in possession of the books (for example, ASIC), can inspect, copy, or take extracts from, the books under s 37(3) of the ASIC Act. The books may also:

- be used in proceedings – s 37(4),
- be retained as long as necessary in the particular circumstances, which may include commencing proceedings – s 37(5), and
- prevent another party from taking a lien over the books – s 37(6).

Under s 37(7)(a) of the ASIC Act, the party in possession *must* allow another party (X) to inspect the books, where X is entitled to do so i.e. perhaps because X is the original holder of the books, and *may* allow a third party to inspect, s 37(7)(b) of the ASIC Act. Hence, s 37(7)(a) is a statutory obligation, whereas s 37(7)(b) is a statutory discretion. It appears that ss 37(5)(a) and 37(7) of the ASIC Act may interact to prevent ASIC from retaining books indefinitely under s 37(5)(a), so that s 37(7) can apply.

The party in possession of the books may require an explanation from the party who produced the books, as to their compilation, s 37(9) of the ASIC Act. There are **exceptions** to the use of books under s 37, where those books have been seized under warrant, s 37(1A) of the ASIC Act.

Section 38 of the ASIC Act outlines powers where **books are not produced**, in that a party (A) fails to comply with an order to produce books. The party seeking the books (B) may request A to state where the books may be found and the location of the party who last had custody or control of the books. ASIC can then use s 33 to require production of the books. A party has "custody and control" of books if they have ability to produce them. It is important to note that more than one party may have "custody or control" i.e. where one party has physical control and the other, legal control. Once a notice has been provided to the party with physical control, the party with legal control may not remove the books i.e. the notice essentially operates as a "freeze": *Federal Commissioner of Taxation v Australia and New Zealand Banking Group Ltd* (1977 – 1979) 143 CLR 499. A statutory duty to produce books prevails over any contractual duty not to produce them.

Power to identify property

Under s 39 of the ASIC Act, a party who may be required to produce company books, may also be required to identify property of the company and explain how the company keeps account of that property. A request to identify and account for property can be exercised even if the party has not been asked to produce the books i.e. the powers operate independent of each other.

Books relating to registered schemes

Section 39A of the ASIC Act permits ASIC to provide to another party, copies of any books relating to registered schemes in its possession, s 39A(1) of the ASIC Act. This can be subject to any conditions which ASIC imposes, and which must be adhered to by the party receiving possession, s 39A(2) of the ASIC Act.

Notifying auditor of foreign regulator access to books

Under s 39B of the ASIC Act, if ASIC has, under s 30A of the Act, obtained books from an auditor under a joint inspection process, and has passed that information to a foreign regulatory body, such as the United States Public Company Accounting Oversight Board (PCAOB), ASIC must inform the auditor of the information which has been passed on. ASIC must make the disclosure in the circumstances as outlined in ss 39B(1)(a) – (d) of the ASIC Act. If ASIC has provided books to a foreign regulatory body pursuant to a section 11(10) agreement with that body, ASIC must notify the Australian auditor in writing, within 14 days, of the details of the books which have been passed on, s 39B(2) of the ASIC Act.

Books relating to the liquidation or external administration of a company

Under s 39C of the ASIC Act, ASIC may transmit books about the liquidation or external administration of a company, to certain parties, s 39C(1) of the ASIC Act, but subject to the conditions listed in s 39C(3) of the Act which include relevancy and reasonableness, and any confidentiality requirements under s 39C(7). Such books may be transmitted to any of the parties as outlined in s 39C(2), including relevant corporations, administrators, officers, creditors or controllers. ASIC must comply with a detailed process, including providing the party (whose books may be disclosed) with notice in writing, pursuant to s 39C(4) of the ASIC Act, and affording them an opportunity to make a written submission to ASIC, detailing any objections, within 10 business days, s 39C(4)(b), before ASIC can release the books.

Search warrants

Sections 39D – 39I of the ASIC Act document ASIC's role in applying and issuing search warrants. These sections took effect on 18 February 2020 and align ASIC's search warrant powers with those in the Crimes Act. It means that ASIC is not obliged to "forewarn" those under investigation, that a search warrant may be imminent. Otherwise, such advance warning may afford the party under investigation the opportunity to conceal or destroy any evidence of misconduct and hence frustrate the very purpose of the search warrant. The relevant provisions for search warrants are explained below:

Crimes Act provisions to be applied

Section 39D of the ASIC Act defines the Crimes Act provisions to be applied for the purposes of ss 39D – 39I of the ASIC Act. Section 39D(3) of the ASIC Act prescribes the indictable offences to which the Crimes Act applies.

Definitions

Section 39F of the ASIC Act modifies the **definition of evidential material** for the purposes of s 39D(1) of the ASIC Act, by removing the words "or a thing relevant to a summary offence".

Section 39I of the ASIC Act inserts **additional definitions** to s 3C(1) of the Crimes Act for the purposes of s 39D(1) of the ASIC Act. These include (amongst others) definitions of "ASIC", "responsible agency" and "responsible Commissioner".

Who may apply for a search warrant

Section 39G of the ASIC Act extends the definition of who may apply for a search warrant to include a member of ASIC.

Use of items obtained via a search warrant

Section 39H of the ASIC Act modifies how items, obtained via a search warrant under the ASIC Act, may be used or shared. This ensures that the purposes, of how items can be used or shared, can be tailored to ASIC's specific processes and needs.

¶7-030 Requirements to Disclose Information and ASIC's Role

Sections 40 – 48 of the ASIC Act provide for the disclosure of information broadly relating to financial products. It is an offence for a party, without reasonable excuse, to fail to comply with a requirement made under ss 41, 42 and 43 of the ASIC Act. The provisions are detailed below.

Restrictions on ASIC

Section 40 of the ASIC Act restricts the right of ASIC to exercise its powers under ss 41 and 42 of the ASIC Act. These restrictions include:

- for the performance of ASIC functions,
- to ensure compliance with the ASIC Act or the Corporations Act,
- for a suspected breach of the ASIC Act or the Corporations Act, or
- for the purposes of investigation.

Similar restrictions apply in s 28 of the ASIC Act in the context of ASIC issuing a notice for inspection of books.

Acquisitions and disposals of financial products

Under s 41 of the ASIC Act, ASIC may require a party who carries on a financial services business to disclose information concerning the acquisitions and disposals of financial products by the business. This may include disclosing details of another party (their name and the nature of instructions provided) where that other party effected the acquisition or disposal, s 41(1)(aa) of the ASIC Act.

Section 41(2) of the ASIC Act imposes disclosure obligations on trustees, namely details of the other party, on whose behalf the trustee acted, and the nature of any instructions provided by the trustee to that other party. Section 41(3) of the ASIC Act imposes obligations on a party who conducts a financial market to disclose the names of parties who acted in acquisition or disposal of financial products on that market; likewise in s 41(4) of the ASIC Act in relation to a clearing and settlement facility.

Acquisition and disposal of trust property

Section 42 of the ASIC Act empowers ASIC to require a trustee company to disclose certain information about acquisition and disposal of trust property by the company. This may include details of a party from whom, or to whom, trust property was acquired or disposed, the nature of any instructions from another party, and details of trust beneficiaries.

ASIC disclosure powers in relation to financial products

Under s 43 of the ASIC Act, ASIC may require a company director, or senior officer, to disclose information in relation to a dealing, or potential dealing in a financial product, s 43(2) of the ASIC Act. However, ASIC can only make this request, under s 43(1) of the ASIC Act, if ASIC believes:

- it may be necessary to prohibit trading in particular financial products,
- a breach of certain provisions of the Corporations Act may have occurred, including unacceptable circumstances within the meaning of Pt 6.9 of the Corporations Act,
- a breach of a Commonwealth, State or Territory Act may have occurred which involves fraud or dishonesty in relation to financial products.

Additional restrictions to ASIC's powers are outlined in s 43(4) of the ASIC Act. If ss 43(1)(a) – (f) of the ASIC Act are satisfied, ASIC may request information relating to dealings in a financial product, financial position, advise, analysis or a report (including an audit report), ss 43(3)(a) – (e) of the ASIC Act. Failure to comply with s 43 of the ASIC Act is an offence of strict liability, unless the party (from which information was requested) has a reasonable excuse, s 63(5) of the ASIC Act.

ASIC disclosure powers in relation to trust property

Under s 44 of the ASIC Act, ASIC may require a company director or senior officer of a trustee company to disclose information which may have affected an acquisition or disposal of trust property, s 44(2) of the ASIC Act. However, ASIC can only make this request if ASIC believes that a breach of a Commonwealth, State or Territory Act may have occurred which involves fraud or dishonesty in relation to trust property, section 44(1) of the ASIC Act. If s 44(1) is satisfied, ASIC may request information relating to the acquisition or disposal of trust property, the financial position of the trust company or an audit report, s 44(3) of the ASIC Act.

ASIC must exercise its powers under this section exclusively for the purpose of investigating the suspected contravention described in s 44(1) of the ASIC Act, and for no other purpose, s 44(4). Failure to comply with s 44 of the ASIC Act is an offence of strict liability, unless the party (from which information was requested) has a reasonable excuse, s 63(5) of the ASIC Act.

Disclosures must take place in private

Section 47 of the ASIC Act refers to disclosures which take place under ss 40 – 48 of the ASIC Act. Such disclosures must take place in private, and ASIC may give directions as to who may be present at a disclosure, s 47(1) of the ASIC Act. Those who are permitted to be present are listed in section 47(2) of the ASIC Act and may include the party's lawyer, s 47(2)(c) of the ASIC Act. Any unauthorised party who is present, is liable, where the offence is one of strict liability, s 47(3) of the ASIC Act.

Legal representation

Section 48 of the ASIC Act permits the lawyer of a party making a disclosure to attend the disclosure and to address ASIC about the disclosure, at such time(s) as ASIC determines, s 48(1) of the ASIC Act. However, s 48(1) does not apply if the presiding representative believes that the lawyer is trying to obstruct or sabotage the examination, s 48(2) of the ASIC Act. ASIC may have the power to exclude a *particular* lawyer, notwithstanding that lawyer's express right to be present: *ASC v Bell* (1991) 9 ACLC 1,606.

¶7-040 ASIC's Role in Proceedings Brought After an Investigation

Sections 49 and 50 of the ASIC Act apply to proceedings brought after an investigation under Pt 3 of the ASIC Act. The provisions are detailed below.

ASIC may commence criminal proceedings

Under s 49 of the ASIC Act, ASIC may commence criminal proceedings if, following investigation or examination, it appears that an offence may have been committed against the ASIC Act or the Corporations Act and the offending party ought to be prosecuted, s 49(1) of the ASIC Act.

ASIC may require the reasonable assistance of parties if ASIC believes on reasonable grounds that the party can assist, or the offence relates to matters connected with a body corporate, s 49(3) of the ASIC Act. ASIC must notify such parties in writing. Section 49(4) of the ASIC Act preserves the privilege against self-incrimination by not obliging the offending party themselves to assist under s 49(3).

Prosecution will normally be conducted by the Commonwealth Director of Public Prosecutions, and operation of the *Director of Public Prosecutions Act 1983 (Cth)* is preserved under s 49(5) of the ASIC Act. *ASC v McLeod* (2000) 18 ACLC 424 held that, under ss 49(2) and 11(4) of the ASIC Act, ASIC is empowered to institute and carry on a prosecution, and do whatever is necessary in connection with prosecution, including the power for ASIC to appeal a decision.

A s 49 decision to prosecute *need not necessarily* be deferred until a final investigation report i.e. it can occur after a record of examination or an interim report: *Hugall v McCusker (No 2)* (1990) 8 ACLC 659. A section 49 decision to prosecute is also not reviewable by the Administrative Appeals Tribunal: *Toll v ASC* (1993) 11 ACLC 226 because a defendant still retains their legal rights under the prosecution: *Schlaepfer v ASIC* [2017] FCA 1122.

ASIC may also commence prosecution if reasonably justified, even if the prosecution does not stem from ASIC investigative or examination powers under Pt 3 of the ASIC Act: *Smolarek v Roper* (2009) 233 FLR 241.

ASIC may commence civil proceedings

Under s 50 of the ASIC Act, ASIC may, following investigation or examination, commence civil proceedings in the name of the party aggrieved, if those proceedings are **in the public interest**. The power under s 50 of the ASIC Act arises once an investigation commences. However, the power does not extend to intervening in existing proceedings begun by other parties: *Carey v ASIC* (2008) 26 ACLC 770.

ASIC cannot claim legal professional privilege for documents brought into existence *before* a decision to commence s 50 proceedings, because there is no client (for a solicitor-client relationship) until proceedings *have* commenced: *Somerville & Ors v Australian Securities Commission & Ors* (1995) 13 ACLC 1. A s 50 decision to commence proceedings is reviewable. However, courts are unlikely to interfere if ASIC has taken an honest view of the facts, its actions are in good faith and the decision does not confer, alter or affect rights: *Rawson Finances Pty Ltd v Cmr of Taxation* (2010) 189 FCR 189. However, there must be a causative link between ASIC's investigation and its conclusion that it is in the public interest to commence proceedings: *Somerville & Ors v Australian Securities Commission & Ors* (1995) 13 ACLC 1.

Proceedings may be for common law damages, recovery of debt or breach of a trust: *Walsh & Ors v Permanent Trustee Australia Ltd & Ors* (1996) 14 ACLC 1. ASIC remains responsible for the cost of proceedings on its part. ASIC may also commence civil penalty proceedings under the Pt 9.4B offence provisions of the Corporations Act, following an investigation under Pt 3 of the ASIC Act: *ASIC v Plymin & Ors (No 2)* (2002) 20 ACLC 1.

¶7-050 ASIC's Role in Audit Deficiency Notifications and Reports

Sections 50A – 50E the ASIC Act permit ASIC to publish an audit deficiency report in relation to specified failures by an Australian auditor. These sections followed enactment of the *Corporations Legislation Amendment (Audit Enhancement) Act 2012 (Cth)*, which commenced on 27 June 2012; hence, ASIC can take action in relation to any audit deficiency identified after that date, s 294 of the ASIC Act. The applicable provisions are summarised below:

Identified audit deficiency

Section 50A of the ASIC Act sets out the circumstances under which ASIC may identify an audit deficiency. An audit deficiency can relate to specific failures by an audit firm which ASIC identified during investigation or the exercise of its statutory audit functions, s 50A(2) of the ASIC Act. ASIC must reasonably believe such failures indicate weakness in the Australian auditor's quality control system or conduct of the audit itself and may be detrimental to the overall quality of the audit, s 50A(1)(c) of the ASIC Act.

Deficiencies may include failure to comply with auditing standards, applicable codes of professional conduct, or audit provisions under the Corporations Act, including those dealing with auditor independence, ss 50A(b)(i) – (iv) of the ASIC Act. An identified audit deficiency may form the basis of an audit deficiency report under s 50C of the ASIC Act.

Notice of audit deficiency

Under s 50B of the ASIC Act, ASIC *may*, but is not obliged to, notify the auditor in writing of an audit deficiency, s 50B(1) of the ASIC Act. The notice must set out the deficiency and any remedial action which ASIC believes is necessary, s 50B(2) of the ASIC Act.

ASIC must invite the auditor to make written submissions to ASIC, within 6 months, about any remedial action which the auditor proposes to undertake. Note that the term "invite" implies that there is no direct statutory compulsion imposed on the auditor in this respect. However, it is the auditor's best interests to prepare submissions for the purposes of ASIC's report, which may be made public.

Audit deficiency report

Section 50C of the ASIC Act states that, once the 6-month period for submissions has expired, ASIC may prepare an audit deficiency report if ASIC is satisfied that the Australian auditor has not taken appropriate action to remedy the audit deficiency, s 50C(1) of the ASIC Act. This may be the case if:

- the auditor has failed to respond to ASIC in any respect,
- the auditor has responded but failed to take any remedial steps, or
- the auditor has taken remedial steps which are inappropriate.

The report must set out the audit deficiency and recommended remedial action as well as any attempts by the auditor to take that action, s 50C(2) of the

ASIC Act. Before preparing the report, ASIC must also take into account any submissions received from the auditor, s 50C(3)(a) of the ASIC Act.

Publication of an audit deficiency report

Section 50D of the ASIC Act permits ASIC, subject to s 50E, to publish an audit deficiency report if ASIC believes it appropriate to do so, s 50D(1) of the ASIC Act. Sections 50D(2) and (3) protect the individual identity of members of the audit team, the subject of the report, as well as the identity of the audited firm.

A decision by ASIC to publish an audit deficiency report is not reviewable by the Administrative Appeals Tribunal. The rationale behind this is that most audit firms comply with their obligations and assist ASIC where adherence to those obligations is shown to be lacking. The threat of publication of an adverse audit report is, in itself, a powerful incentive for audit firms to comply, and take remedial action where required. The statutory process under ss 50A – 50E of the ASIC Act also affords audit firms sufficient opportunity for their case to be heard.

Section 50E of the ASIC Act provides for **consultation before publication** of an audit deficiency report. This consultation requires ASIC to provide the auditor, who is the subject of the report, with a copy, and invite the auditor to provide their comments within 21 days, s 50E(1) of the ASIC Act. If the report is then subsequently published, it must include any comments, as received from the auditor, s 50E(2) of the ASIC Act.

¶7-060 ASIC's Role in Hearings

The power to hold hearings or conduct proceedings is exercised by ASIC (under Pt 3, Div 6 of the ASIC Act), the Takeovers Panel (under Pt 10 of the ASIC Act), and the Companies Auditors Disciplinary Board (under Pt 11 of the ASIC Act).

It should be noted that this publication is concerned only with ASIC hearings, so that the provisions relating to the Takeovers Panel and the Companies Auditors Disciplinary Board are beyond the scope of this publication. Having said that, the provisions to govern the conduct of a hearing, including the submission of evidence, handling of witnesses and contempt of proceedings, are similar for all three bodies. The ASIC provisions are described below.

Power to hold hearings

Section 51 of the ASIC Act conveys ASIC with the power to hold hearings for the exercise of any of its functions under the ASIC Act or the Corporations Act, except for **excluded** provisions (s 12A and Pt 2, Div 2, ss 12AC – 12HD of the ASIC Act, relating to unconscionable conduct and consumer protection in financial services). The s 51 exclusions also extend to sections 657C and 657G of the Corporations Act (which relate to the Takeovers Panel making a declaration of unacceptable circumstances). The term "hearing" should not be given any technical or formal meaning: *NCSC v The News Corporation Ltd & Ors* (1984) 2 ACLC 301.

Public and private hearings

Under s 52 of the ASIC Act, and subject to ss 53 and 54, ASIC may direct that a hearing take place in public or in private, s 52(1) of the ASIC Act. In exercising this discretion, ASIC must, under s 52(2) of the ASIC Act, consider whether:

- any evidence or matter, which may arise during a hearing, is confidential or relates to the commission, or suspected commission, of an offence, and
- unfair prejudice to the defendant's reputation is likely if a public hearing takes place, and
- it is in the public interest to hold a public hearing.

ASIC's express s 52 power to conduct a private hearing, carries with it an implied power to take all reasonable steps to ensure that the hearing is indeed private; for example, by issuing a "non-disclosure order": *NCSC v Bankers Trust Australia Ltd & Ors* (1990) 8 ACLC 1.

Public hearings

Under s 53 of the ASIC Act, and subject to s 54, a party to appear at an ASIC hearing may request that the hearing take place in public and ASIC must comply with their wishes, s 53(1) of the ASIC Act. However, under s 53(2) of the ASIC Act, ASIC may direct that the hearing be conducted in private if ASIC is satisfied that it should be, having regard to the matters in s 52(2) of the ASIC Act.

Private hearings

Under s 54 of the ASIC Act, if the ASIC Act and the Corporations Act (except for the excluded provisions), requires an ASIC hearing to take place in private, then it must take place in private. The excluded provisions refer to s 12A and Pt 2, Div 2, ss 12AC – 12HD of the ASIC Act, relating to unconscionable conduct and consumer protection in financial services.

ASIC may restrict publication of evidence

Under s 55 of the ASIC Act, ASIC may prevent or restrict publication of evidence, or matters in documents as lodged with ASIC, s 55(1) of the ASIC Act. In exercising this discretion, ASIC must, under s 55(2) of the ASIC Act, consider whether:

- any evidence or matter, which may arise during a hearing, is confidential or relates to the commission, or the suspected commission, of an offence, and
- any unfair prejudice to the defendant's reputation is likely if publication takes place, and
- it is in the public interest to publish the evidence, or matter.

The term "publication" does not encompass production of evidence. Hence, ASIC directions preventing publication of evidence do not prevent that evidence being produced to the court under a subpoena or a notice to produce: *Potts v Dennis Jones & Co Pty Ltd & Ors (No 2)* (1995) 13 ACLC 1.

Attendance at a private hearing

Under s 56 of the ASIC Act, ASIC may give directions as to who may be present at a private hearing, s 56(1) of the ASIC Act. Those who are permitted to be present are listed in ss 56(2) and (3) of the ASIC Act. Any unauthorised party who is present, is liable for breach of s 56 of the ASIC Act, where the offence is one of strict liability, ss 56(3) and (4) of the ASIC Act.

Requirements at hearings

Section 57 of the ASIC Act states that a party to appear at a hearing must be given **written notice of the hearing**, including the place and time for attendance, s 57(2) of the ASIC Act. If the party does not wish to appear, they may lodge **written submissions** with ASIC which they wish to have considered in the matter, s 57(3) of the ASIC Act.

Witnesses and evidence

Section 58 of the ASIC Act permits ASIC to summon witnesses to provide evidence or produce specified documents, section 58(1) of the ASIC Act. Evidence may be taken on oath or affirmation, s 58(2), the purpose of which is to ensure that the evidence given will be true, s 58(3) of the ASIC Act.

A witness must answer questions put to them, whilst a person appearing pursuant to a summons must produce the document(s) as specified in the summons, s 58(4) of the ASIC Act. A witness may also be permitted to give evidence by tendering a written statement, which must be verified on oath if required by ASIC, s 58(5) of the ASIC Act. Failure to comply with s 58 of the ASIC Act is an offence of strict liability, s 58(4A).

A party who has attended a hearing at the request of ASIC, or pursuant to a summons, is entitled to be paid the prescribed allowances and expenses (if any), as ASIC believes to be reasonable, ss 89(2) and (3) of the ASIC Act.

Format of hearings

Section 59 of the ASIC Act states that hearings must be conducted with as **little formality**, and with as much expediency, as permissible, s 59(1) of the ASIC Act. Indeed, s 59(3) treats the hearing akin to an ASIC meeting. ASIC is **not bound by the rules of evidence** and may permit another party to intervene, s 59(2) of the ASIC Act.

In contrast to adversarial hearings (which affect a party's rights and hence entitle a party to be present), strict adherence to the rules of natural justice is not required in inquisitorial hearings, such as those run by ASIC. This means that a witness may be adequately represented, in some cases, by their lawyer: *NCSC v The News Corporation Ltd & Ors* (1984) 2 ACLC 301. Similarly, a party may appear in person or be represented by their employee, s 59(5) of the ASIC Act.

All parties are entitled to **legal representation**, s 59(8) of the ASIC Act. However, ASIC may refuse to permit a *particular* legal representative to appear, if it reasonably believes on good faith, that the representation will, or may, prejudice the matter, for example by representing more than one witness: *Wood v NCSC* (1990) 8 ACLC 462. Likewise, in *Fiorentino v Companies Auditors and Liquidators Disciplinary Board* [2014] FCA 641, denial of legal representation did not amount to a denial of natural justice where the defendant was sufficiently educated to allow for self-representation. Hence, much will turn on the particular circumstances of each case.

ASIC must consider evidence and submissions

Section 60 of the ASIC Act makes it clear that ASIC must take account of any evidence or submissions, as provided by the parties, when making a decision on a matter.

Refer questions of law

Section 61 of the ASIC Act permits ASIC, of its own motion or at a party's request, to refer questions of law to a court, s 61(1) of the ASIC Act. While a question of law is pending, ASIC must not make a decision or proceed in a manner which is inconsistent with the court, s 61(3) of the ASIC Act. ASIC must provide the court with all relevant documents; these documents will be returned by the court to ASIC once the question of law is determined, s 61(4) of the ASIC Act.

Protection of hearing participants

Section 62 of the ASIC Act confers the same protection and immunity in High Court proceedings to ASIC's members, witnesses, and legal representatives, in conducting ASIC hearings. Under s 62(1A) of the ASIC Act, an ASIC delegate will have the same immunity as an ASIC member.

¶7-070 Offences

Sections 63 – 70 of the ASIC Act list several offences for breach of provisions relating to the operations of ASIC, the Takeovers Panel (Pt 10, Div 3 of the ASIC Act), and the Companies Auditors Disciplinary Board (Pt 11, Div 2 of the ASIC Act).

It should be noted that this publication is concerned only with ASIC offences, so that the offence provisions for the Takeovers Panel and the Companies Auditors Disciplinary Board are beyond the scope of this publication. Having said that, all 3 bodies prescribe similar offences. The ASIC offence provisions are described below.

Non-compliance

Section 63 of the ASIC Act makes it clear that a party must not, without reasonable excuse, explanation or statement, fail to comply with the provisions as listed in s 63 of the ASIC Act. The offences listed carry different penalties – either penalty units or imprisonment.

In *CAC v Yuill & Ors* (1991) 9 ACLC 843, the term "reasonable excuse" was held to be any physical or practical difficulties in complying with a requirement; however, it did not extend to legal professional privilege. Likewise, in *ASC v Zarro & Ors* (1992) 10 ACLC 11, a confidentiality obligation was rejected as constituting a "reasonable excuse" for non-compliance with a requirement to produce documents; see also *Australian Securities Commission v Ampolex Ltd & Ors* (1996) 14 ACLC 80. However, the "physical and practical difficulties" argument was rejected in *Australian Securities and Investments Commission v Albarran* (2008) 169 FCR 448. What constitutes a "reasonable excuse" turns very much on the particular circumstances of each case: *Bank of Valletta PLC v National Crime Authority* [1999] FCA 791. There is a need to balance the adverse consequences on the party obliged to comply, against the adverse consequences (for example, on an investigation) if that party fails to comply. The expense, inconvenience or burden of complying with a provision of the ASIC Act, will not ordinarily provide a reasonable excuse for non-compliance: *Maxi EFX Global AU Pty Ltd v ASIC* [2021] FCAFC 59.

Section 70 of the ASIC Act outlines the **powers of the court for non-compliance** with Pt 3 of the ASIC Act (except for Div 8). If ASIC is satisfied that a party has, without reasonable excuse, failed to comply, s 70(1) of the ASIC Act permits ASIC to certify that failure to the court, s 70(2) of the ASIC Act. This permits the court to inquire into, and order a party to comply with the requirement, s 70(3) of the ASIC Act. The meaning of the term *"reasonable excuse"* is discussed in *CAC of NSW v Yuill & Ors* (1991) 9 ACLC 843, above.

Certification by ASIC, pursuant to s 70(2) of the ASIC Act, enables the court to inquire into the case, but does not oblige it to do so: *Insurance and Superannuation Commissioner v Glaser* (1997) 79 FCR 505. However, certification generally provides a sufficient reason for the court to conduct the contemplated inquiry into whether the notice had been complied with: *Maxi EFX Global AU Pty Ltd v ASIC* (2021) 284 FCR 643; (2021) 152 ACSR 106; [2021] FCAFC 59.

False information

Under s 64 of the ASIC Act, a party must not provide information, or make a statement, which is false or misleading in a material particular. This applies under examination: *DPP (Cth) v Couper* [2013] VSCA 72 (conviction for a white collar crime), in compliance with a Pt 3 requirement, s 64(1), or at a hearing, s 64(2). However, s 64(3) of the ASIC Act provides a defence if the defendant can prove that, at the time of providing the information, they believed on reasonable grounds that it was true and not misleading, s 64(3).

Obstructing or hindering

Section 65 of the ASIC Act states that a party must not obstruct or hinder another party exercising power under Pt 3 of the ASIC Act, s 65(1). However, s 65(1A) provides a defence if the defendant can prove that they had a "reasonable excuse". The term "reasonable excuse" is discussed in the context of non-compliance under s 63 of the ASIC Act, above. The term "obstruct or hinder" may mean conduct which is "essentially negative in character", for example the retention of documents indefinitely: *Re: Ansett Transport Industries (Operations) Pty Ltd and: Australian Federation of Air Pilots* (1991) 30 FCR 183.

Contempt of ASIC

Section 66 of the ASIC Act makes it clear that a party must not obstruct or hinder ASIC in the performance of their functions, s 66(1)(a) of the ASIC Act, or disrupt an ASIC hearing, s 66(1)(b) of the ASIC Act. Under s 66(2) of the ASIC Act, a party must not breach an ASIC direction, under s 55, to restrict publication of evidence, unless the party has a reasonable excuse to do so, s 66(2A) of the ASIC Act.

Concealing books

Section 67 of the ASIC Act states that where ASIC is investigating, or about to investigate, a matter, a party must not conceal, destroy, mutilate or alter a book relating to that matter, s 67(1)(a), or send the book interstate or overseas, s 67(1)(b). Under s 67(2) of the ASIC Act, it is a defence if the defendant can prove that they did not intend to breach the ASIC Act or the Corporations Act, or to delay or obstruct an ASIC investigation. "Books" are broadly defined in s 5(1) of the ASIC Act, to include a document, register, account, accounting record, banker's book, and "any other record" of information.

Self-incrimination

Broadly speaking, the common law privilege against self-incrimination is revoked by s 68(1) of the ASIC Act. However, s 68(3) of the ASIC Act then goes on to provide that a statement made, or the fact that a party (X) has signed a record, in accordance with a requirement under the ASIC Act, is not admissible as evidence against X in subsequent criminal proceedings or proceedings for the imposition of a penalty, where X has made it clear that the statement or record may tend to incriminate them, s 68(2) of the ASIC Act. Hence, s 68(2) offers some relief against self-incrimination. However, evidence will be admissible if the proceeding relates to the falsity of a statement or any record, ss 68(3)(c) and (d) of the ASIC Act.

In *Rich & Anor v ASIC* (2004) 22 ACLC 1, "proceedings for the imposition of a penalty" included a banning order against a financial services provider. However, this High Court decision led to the enactment of s 1349 of the Corporations Act, which removed penalty privilege for proceedings where a disqualification, banning, suspension or cancellation order is sought. In *R v Catena (No 3)* [2013] WASC 97, the court held that providing a prosecutor with an examination transcript, under s 19 of the ASIC Act, is not, in itself, likely to prejudice the fair trial of a defendant who has claimed privilege over that transcript, pursuant to s 68 of the ASIC Act. The privilege against self-incrimination, in s 68 of the ASIC Act, cannot be claimed to avoid disclosing a party's defence to a charge: *Hamilton v Oades; CAC v Oades & Anor* (1989) 7 ACLC 381. Likewise, the claim is not available on the grounds that it may incriminate others: *NCSC v Sim (No 3)* (1987) 5 ACLC 500 (in relation to an officer and a corporation); however, it may be available if the officer may also be incriminated by the statements; for example, in aiding or abetting the principal offence.

Legal professional privilege

Under s 69 of the ASIC Act, if a party requires a lawyer to give information or produce a book which would disclose privileged client-solicitor communications, s 69(1) of the ASIC Act, then the lawyer is entitled to refuse to comply unless the client agrees to the lawyer complying with the requirement, s 69(2) of the ASIC Act. If the lawyer refuses, under s 69(2), they must as soon as practicable, provide to the party requesting the information, the name and address of the client (if known), and sufficient particulars to identify the information or book requested, ss 69(3)(a) – (c) of the ASIC Act.

Legal professional privilege is a fundamental doctrine which is not to be revoked except in the clearest terms: *Corporate Affairs Commission (NSW) v Yuill & Ors* (1991) 9 ACLC 843. It serves the public interest in the administration of justice by encouraging full and frank disclosure between clients and their lawyers: *Esso Australia Resources Limited v The Commissioner of Taxation* [1999] HCA 67. However, courts must also have full access to the relevant facts and evidence. Hence, a balance is required, and legal professional privilege is necessarily confined. The High Court in *Esso Australia Resources Limited v The Commissioner of Taxation* [1999] HCA 67 adopted the broader **dominant purpose test** as the appropriate common law test for privilege. This replaced the sole purpose test, established by the High Court in *Grant v Downs* (1975-1976) 135 CLR 674, but which was considered too narrow. The practical implication of overriding legal professional privilege is that ASIC may be unduly assisted in their case against a corporation by gaining access to that corporations legal advice.

¶7-080 ASIC's Powers where Non-Compliance with Part 3 of the ASIC Act

ASIC's powers under ss 71 – 75 of the ASIC Act are intended as interim measures to preserve the status quo of an investigation, essentially as "orders of a protective or preservative nature". Hence, they are not intended to be used over prolonged periods of time during a lengthy investigation: *Centurion Trust Company Ltd v ASIC* (2004) 22 ACLC 223. Having said that, the ASIC Act does not place any express time limitation on these powers.

Other "orders of a protective or preservative nature" are contained in ss 1323 and 1324 of the Corporations Act. The provisions for ASIC to deal with non-compliance, with Pt 3 of the ASIC Act, are detailed below.

Orders

Section 71 of the ASIC Act empowers ASIC to make several orders relating to:

- affairs of a body corporate – s 71(a),
- financial products – s 71(b), or
- trust property acquired, or disposed of, by a trustee company – s 71(c).

ASIC may make the orders, as outlined in s 71 of the ASIC Act, if the information concerning these matters cannot be obtained because a party has failed to comply with a requirement under Pt 3 of the ASIC Act.

Orders relating to securities of a body corporate

If s 71(a) of the ASIC Act is satisfied then, under s 72 of the ASIC Act, ASIC may make orders restraining a specified party from acquiring, or disposing of, security interests or exercising voting rights in relation to the body corporate in question, ss 72(1)(a) – (c) of the ASIC Act. ASIC may also direct the body corporate itself not to pay a sum in respect of specific securities (except in winding up) and not to register the transfer of securities or issue shares, ss 72(1)(e) – (g) of the ASIC Act.

Restraining the disposal of security interests, under s 72(1)(a) of the ASIC Act, can be limited to particular purchasers or shares. However, ASIC cannot impose conditions which operate *after* the sale: *Centurion Trust Co Ltd v ASIC* (2003) 21 ACLC 275. The "specified" party, in s 72(1)(a) and (b) of the ASIC Act, does not have to be the same party who failed to comply with Pt 3 of the ASIC Act, as to do so would severely impede ASIC's powers to remedy non-compliance with investigation and information-gathering powers: *Centurion Trust Co Ltd v ASIC* (2003) 21 ACLC 275.

Orders relating to financial products and trust property,

If s 71(b) of the ASIC Act is satisfied then, under s 73 of the ASIC Act, ASIC may make orders restraining a specified party from acquiring or disposing of any interests in specific financial products or exercising voting rights in relation to specified financial products, ss 73(1)(a) – (c) of the ASIC Act. ASIC may also direct a body corporate not to pay a sum in respect of specific financial products (except in winding up) and not to register the transfer of a financial product or issue shares, ss 73(1)(e) – (g) of the ASIC Act.

If s 71(c) of the ASIC Act is satisfied then, under s 73 of the ASIC Act, ASIC may also make orders restraining a specified party from acquiring or disposing of any interests in specific trust property, ss 73(1A)(a) and (b) of the ASIC Act. ASIC may also direct a body corporate not to pay a sum in respect of specific trust property (except in winding up) and not to register the transfer of specific trust property, ss 73(1A)(c) and (d) of the ASIC Act.

Orders under ss 73(1) or (1A) of the ASIC Act do not prevent the operator of a financial market or clearing/settlement facility, from closing out, or transferring, a derivative, ss 73(2)(a) and (b) of the ASIC Act.

Making and varying orders

This is governed by s 75 of the ASIC Act. Orders under ss 72 and 73 are made by publishing a notice in the *Gazette*, s 75(2) of the ASIC Act. ASIC must give to the party, to whom the order is directed, a copy of the order and any order varying or revoking it, s 75(3) of the ASIC Act. If an order relates to financial products, ASIC must give a copy of the order to the financial product owner or the party against which any right or option is enforceable, s 75(4) of the ASIC Act.

An order can be varied or revoked by a later order, s 75(1) of the ASIC Act. However, this does not expand the scope of ASIC's powers, as any varying order under s 75 of the ASIC Act continues to be an order under ss 72 and 73 of the Act, and hence cannot be greater in scope: *Centurion Trust Co Ltd v ASIC* (2003) 21 ACLC 275.

¶7-090 ASIC's Evidentiary Use of Certain Material

Subject to any express limitations, ss 76 – 83 of the ASIC Act permit evidence gained from examinations and hearings to be used in court or tribunal "proceedings", which includes civil, criminal, administrative or disciplinary proceedings, s 5(1) of the ASIC Act. The provisions govern the admissibility into evidence of certain materials including examination statements, certified copies of ASIC investigation reports and books relating to:

- the affairs of a body corporate
- audit matters
- a financial market or settlement / clearing facility
- financial advice and reports
- the financial position of a body corporate.

The purpose and scope of the provisions were described in *ASIC v Singapore Liason Pty Ltd* [1998] FCA 1813 as a complete "code" (in their own right) to supplement the other means available to adduce evidence: *Australian Securities and Investments Commission (ASIC) v Activesuper Pty Ltd (in liq)* [2015] FCA 342. These evidentiary provisions are detailed below.

Examination statements and proceedings against examinee

Under s 76 of the ASIC Act, statements made by a party at an examination are admissible in evidence against that party in a proceeding. However, this is qualified by the **exceptions** outlined in ss 76(1)(a) – (d) of the ASIC Act, including:

- the common law right against self-incrimination – s 68 of the ASIC Act,
- the statement is not relevant to the proceeding,
- the statement must be qualified or explained by some other statement at the examination, or
- the party can claim legal professional privilege in respect of the statement.

Legal professional privilege is discussed in the context of s 69 of the ASIC Act, above, and discussed in the High Court case of *Corporate Affairs Commission (NSW) v Yuill & Ors* (1991) 9 ACLC 843.

The provisions of s 76(1) of the ASIC Act are also applicable in **joint proceedings**, i.e. where a proceeding is heard together with another party's proceeding, s 76(2) of the ASIC Act. A signed record of examination is *prima facie* evidence of the statements it records; however, the admissibility of other examination statements is not limited by Pt 3 of the ASIC Act, s 76(3) of the ASIC Act. Hence, a taped interview may be subject to the common law, but not Pt 3 of the ASIC Act.

Evidence of absent witnesses

Section 77 of the ASIC Act permits a party's evidence (which *would* be admissible) to be admitted by means of a statement, where that party (the "absent witness") cannot provide evidence directly to the court or tribunal. The reasons for non-attendance at the court or tribunal may be because the absent witness is deceased, unfit, outside the State or Territory or unable to be located after all reasonable steps have been taken to locate them, ss 77(a)(i) – (iii) of the ASIC Act.

Sections 76 and 77 of the ASIC Act often afford the primary means for the admission of such statements, but this is not always the case: *ASIC v Fortescue Metals Group Ltd (No 2)* [2009] FCA 424.

Weight of the evidence

Section 78 of the ASIC Act sets out the criteria for measuring the weight of the evidence, which has been provided by an absent witness, and which is admissible under s 77 of the ASIC Act. The criteria under s 78(2)(a) – (c) of the ASIC Act, are:

- the elapsed time between the events or matters and the statement being made,
- any reasons for the absent witness to conceal or misrepresent information, and
- any other circumstances which may impact on the accuracy of the statement.

Where a party is not called as a witness, but that party's evidence would have been admissible to support or destroy their credibility, then that evidence is admissible, s 78(3)(a) of the ASIC Act. Evidence of a party not called as a witness is also admissible to show inconsistency between their statement and another statement they made, s 78(3) of the ASIC Act. However, evidence is not admissible if the party was called as a witness and denied the matter in cross-examination, s 78(4) of the ASIC Act.

Objection to admission of examination statements

Under s 79 of the ASIC Act, a party may object to the admission of examination statements into evidence. The "adducing party" to a proceeding *may*, within 14 days of the hearing, provide to another party to the proceeding written notice that the adducing party will apply to have admitted into evidence specified examination statements, s 79(1) of the ASIC Act. The written notice must include the specified examination statements, s 79(2) of the ASIC Act.

The other party may object to the statements being admitted and provide grounds for those objections, s 79(3) of the ASIC Act. This objection must be made within 14 days of receiving the written notification, unless that period is extended by the court, tribunal or the parties themselves, s 79(4) of the ASIC Act. The adducing party must provide copies of all documents to the court or tribunal, s 79(5) of the ASIC Act, following which the court or tribunal will determine the objections, either before or during the hearing, s 79(6) of the ASIC Act.

Admissibility of books and extracts

Under s 80 of the ASIC Act, a copy of, or extract of, certain books is admissible in evidence, as if it were the original, s 80(1) of the ASIC Act. This applies to books relating to affairs of a body corporate, audit matters, liquidation, financial products and registered schemes, ss 80(1)(a) – (c) of the ASIC Act. To be admissible, the copy or extract must be a true copy or extract, s 80(2) of the ASIC Act and a party who has compared the original against the copy, for the purpose of satisfying s 80(2) of the ASIC Act may give oral or written evidence of that fact, s 80(3) of the ASIC Act.

ASIC report

Section 81 of the ASIC Act allows for an ASIC report to be made under Pt 3, Div 1 of the ASIC Act. Where such a report is certified by ASIC as a true copy, this is *prima facie* evidence of its contents, and the report may be admissible in civil proceedings. The report may contain ASIC's opinion for the purposes of winding up both a company and a non-corporate body, under ss 461(1)(h) and 583(c)(iii) of the Corporations Act respectively. This is due to the fact that ASIC may investigate and report on the inability of a corporate or non-corporate body, to pay their debts, in support of an application for winding up. The onus of disproving the report is then on the party opposing the winding up.

Admissibility of section 81 reports

Section 82 of the ASIC Act qualifies the admissibility of s 81 reports. A s 81 report is not admissible unless the defendant has been provided with a copy of the report and a reasonable opportunity to examine it in preparing their case, s 82(2) of the ASIC Act. The defendant may also apply to cross-examine witnesses who were involved in preparing the report, s 82(3) of the ASIC Act. The court must grant leave for the defendant to apply under s 82(3), unless it is not appropriate to do so, s 82(4) of the ASIC Act.

The court must refuse to admit the report, if the failure of a witness to attend for cross-examination pursuant to s 82(3) of the ASIC Act would unfairly prejudice the defendant, s 82(5) of the ASIC Act.

Evidence otherwise admissible

Section 83 of the ASIC Act states that nothing in Pt 3, Div 9 of the ASIC Act affects the admissibility of evidence in proceedings, if it would otherwise be admissible i.e. except for Div 9. Hence, evidence which would be admissible under the Evidence Act, remains admissible, despite any contrary intention in Pt 3, Div 9 of the ASIC Act.

¶7-100 Miscellaneous Provisions of the ASIC Act – Part 3

Sections 84 – 93AA of the ASIC Act contain miscellaneous provisions which support the operation of Pt 3 of the ASIC Act, but which do not naturally fall under any other part of Pt 3. These miscellaneous provisions are discussed in more detail below.

Lifting the corporate veil

Section 84 of the ASIC Act states that a requirement which can be made of a body corporate under Pt 3 of the ASIC Act can also be made of a party who is an officer of the body. This essentially permits ASIC to "pierce" or "lift the corporate veil" by ensuring that those individuals behind the corporation can be held personally liable.

Authority to act as an ASIC inspector

Under s 85 of the ASIC Act, evidence of a party's authority to act as an ASIC inspector and the scope of that authority must be provided, if the other party so requests. Such evidence may include an identity card, s 85(a) of the ASIC Act, or a written authorisation from ASIC, s 85(b) of the ASIC Act.

Service of documents on natural persons

The Corporations Act s 109X applies to the service of documents on natural persons. Section 86 of the ASIC Act adds a qualification to this provision, when leaving a document at an address.

Time and place for production of books

Section 87 of the ASIC Act ensures that the time and place specified for the production of books is reasonable, s 87(A) of the ASIC Act. If the time and place for production are held to be reasonable, then the party requisitioning the books can require their immediate production, s 87(b) of the ASIC Act.

Application of the Crimes Act and the Evidence Act

Section 88 of the ASIC Act clarifies how the Crimes Act and the Evidence Act apply to Pt 3 of the ASIC Act. An examination or hearing under Pt 3, Div 6 of the ASIC Act is a judicial proceeding under the Crimes Act, Pt III. Part III of the Crimes Act also imposes penalties for a number of offences. The following provisions of the Evidence Act apply to an ASIC *examination* in the same way as to a *proceeding* under s 4 of the Evidence Act:

- Pt 2.2, ss 69, 70, 71, and 147 – Exceptions to the hearsay rule and facilitating proof by the tendering of documents,
- Pt 4.6, Div 2 – Proof of certain matters by affidavits or written statements.

Expenses

Section 89 of the ASIC Act states that allowances and expenses are to be paid to a party appearing at an examination, under s 89(1) of the ASIC Act, or a summons, under s 89(2) of the ASIC Act. ASIC may pay such amount as it thinks reasonable, s 89(3) of the ASIC Act.

Sections 90 and 91 of the ASIC Act deal with the expenses associated with an ASIC investigation. Under s 90 of the ASIC Act, ASIC must pay the expenses of an investigation under Pt 3, Div 1 of the ASIC Act. Section 90 of the ASIC Act does not entitle a third party to recover expenses from ASIC: *Westpac Banking Corporation v Australian Securities Commission* (1997) 15 ACA4C 445.

Under s 91 of the ASIC Act, ASIC may recover investigation expenses from the party convicted, or against whom judgment is awarded, s 91(1) of the ASIC Act. An order for recovery of expenses must be in writing, setting out when and how payment can be made, s 91(2) of the ASIC Act. ASIC may recover any unpaid expenses as a debt, s 91(4) of the ASIC Act.

Operational effect of Part 3 of the ASIC Act

Section 93 of the ASIC Act states that Pt 3 of the ASIC Act does not diminish any other function or power as conferred by a law of the Commonwealth, State or Territory, s 93(2) of the ASIC Act.

¶7-110 ASIC's Use of Enforceable Undertakings

Under sections 93AA and 93A of the ASIC Act, ASIC *may* accept a written "enforceable undertaking" from a party, or the responsible entity of a registered scheme, for any matter over which ASIC has jurisdiction. ASIC may also accept a written undertaking from the operator of a notified foreign passport fund or a corporate collective investment vehicle (CCIV), in relation to which ASIC has a function under the ASIC Act and/or the Corporations Act, ss 93B and 93BA of the ASIC Act.

An enforceable undertaking is essentially a form of **remedy**. It is a consensual settlement agreement and provides an alternative to court action, although ASIC may use enforceable undertakings in conjunction with other actions.

ASIC may also accept an enforceable undertaking while continuing to investigate specific matters outside the enforceable undertaking.

An enforceable undertaking may also produce outcomes which are not available through more formal proceedings. However, ASIC is unlikely to enter into an enforceable undertaking if there is a more effective regulatory outcome. Additionally, if a matter has already been referred to a body ASIC will be reluctant to then accept an enforceable undertaking.

An enforceable undertaking cannot be used in criminal proceedings. The rationale is that a party cannot "contract out" of criminal liability.

AISC Regulatory Guide – RG-100 – *Court enforceable undertakings* – provides further guidance on the use of enforceable undertakings by ASIC.

ASIC's power to accept enforceable undertakings

Sections 93AA – 93BA of the ASIC Act confer on ASIC a power to "accept" enforceable undertakings; hence, ASIC cannot impose or require a party to enter into an enforceable undertaking. Similarly, use of the words "may accept" means that a party cannot require ASIC to accept an enforceable undertaking, although the Administrative Appeals Tribunal, for example, may compel ASIC to accept: *ASIC v Donald* (2002) 20 ACLC 1.

ASIC will generally only accept an enforceable undertaking if it offers a more effective outcome in the circumstances, taking into account community interests and the compliance history of the party seeking the undertaking. In deciding whether to accept an enforceable undertaking, ASIC will consider the defendant's willingness to publicly acknowledge ASIC's concerns and cooperate with ASIC, the scope and impact of the breach and whether it was intentional, and any prior misconduct on the part of the defendant.

Terms of an enforceable undertaking

ASIC will accept an enforceable undertaking only if the defendant commits to stop the alleged breach which concerns ASIC. At a minimum, the following terms are recommended for an enforceable undertaking, although these should be tailored to the individual circumstances of the case.

- **Compliance and monitoring** – How a defendant will address the offending conduct and ensure that it does not reoccur. A defendant must have adequate control and compliance programs for monitoring how the undertaking is implemented, any external assessment or audit of the changes, and for reporting to ASIC.

- **Rectification or compensatory action** – This may involve a defendant compensating or reimbursing parties who have been adversely affected by its misconduct.
- **Corrective notices** – ASIC may require a defendant to explicitly correct any misleading conduct for which it was responsible. Corrective notices provide the means to do this in a public forum.
- **Rights** – A defendant must acknowledge that the enforceable undertaking does not affect the rights of other parties or place any restraint on ASIC, beyond that which is agreed between the parties.

Generally, ASIC will not accept an enforceable undertaking which:

- denies liability,
- fails to include details of the misconduct,
- omits any standard clauses, or
- contains defences for any breach of the undertaking.

ASIC will also not accept an enforceable undertaking in confidence, although ASIC may agree to protect certain information which is personal, commercial or which would be against public interest to disclose, ss 93A(6), 93B(6) and 93CBA(6) of the ASIC Act. If required, either ASIC or the defendant (subject to ASIC consent) may appoint an independent expert, to review the enforceable undertaking and report on certain matters.

Breach of an enforceable undertaking

If ASIC believes that an enforceable undertaking has been breached, it may make an application to the court, under ss 93AA(3) – 93BA(3) of the ASIC Act, for an order. Sections 93AA(4) – 93BA(4) of the ASIC Act permit the court to make several orders in relation to the enforceable undertaking, including an order that the defendant comply with the undertaking, ss 93AA(4)(a) – 93BA(4)(a) of the ASIC Act. This essentially converts a private agreement into a court undertaking, breach of which may constitute contempt of court.

ASIC is not *legally* obliged to notify the defendant of their intention to apply to the court for an order under ss 93AA(4) – 93BA(4) of the ASIC Act. However, a defendant is entitled, under the principles of natural justice, to make representations to the court in support of their case, of which they should have notice. Hence, there is an equitable obligation on ASIC to notify the defendant of any potential proceedings.

Third party interests may also be affected by breach of an undertaking. However, ss 93AA – 93BA of the ASIC Act apply only to the rights or obligations of parties who are privy to the undertaking. Hence, it would be difficult for a third party to seek judicial review of an enforceable undertaking, due to a lack of standing.

¶7-120 Criminal Penalties

The *Treasury Laws Amendment (Strengthening Corporate and Financial Sector Penalties) Act 2019 (Cth)* made significant amendments to the offence and civil penalty provisions of the ASIC Act. The new provisions have been in effect, in full, since 1 January 2021.

A new Pt 3B of the ASIC Act (entitled Criminal penalties) comprises ss 93C – 93H, and is summarised as follows:

Penalty for committing an offence

Section 93C of the ASIC Act provides that a party who is convicted of an offence against the ASIC Act is punishable by a penalty not exceeding the penalty applicable to that offence, s 93C(1) of the ASIC Act. Additionally, if a trustee of a registrable superannuation entity commits an offence against the ASIC Act, and the penalty is, or includes, a fine, then in determining the fine, the court must consider impact of the fine on beneficiaries of the superannuation entity, s 93C(2) of the ASIC Act.

Penalty for an offence committed by an individual or a body corporate

The penalty in this case could be either a fine or imprisonment, ss 93D (for an individual) and 93E (for a body corporate). Section 93D of the ASIC Act provides a formula for calculating the fine payment for an individual in breach.

Meaning of benefit derived and detriment avoided

The terms " benefit derived" and "detriment avoided" are defined in s 93F of the ASIC Act. These terms are used in the calculation of penalties for both individuals, under s 93D of the ASIC Act, and body corporates under s 93E of the ASIC Act.

Penalty specified or not specified

Section 93G of the ASIC Act states that if the penalty for an offence is specified in the provision, then that is the penalty to be applied.

However, under s 93HG of the ASIC Act, if no penalty for an offence is specified, then:

- The offence is an offence of strict liability, and
- A penalty of 20 units applies to the offence.

Chapter 8

MISCELLANEOUS PROVISIONS OF THE ASIC ACT

Sections 243B – 251 of the ASIC Act contain miscellaneous provisions which don't naturally fall under any other part of the ASIC Act.

This chapter outlines and discusses these miscellaneous provisions in the context of ASIC's role.

¶8-000 Offences and Jurisdiction

Section 243B of the ASIC Act states that if a party commits an offence *outside* Australia which, had it been committed within Australia, would be a breach of the ASIC Act, then the party is guilty of that offence.

¶8-010 ASIC may Publish Internal Dispute Resolution Information

Section 243C of the ASIC Act permits ASIC to publish the internal dispute resolution data of corporations. This information may be provided to ASIC under several listed legislation, including the Corporations Act, s 243C(1)(a)(i) of the ASIC Act. This power also extends to information which may be derived from the "original information", s 243C(1)(b) of the ASIC Act. The published information may be capable of identifying a particular entity, but not a particular individual. In other words, protections afforded by the *Privacy Act 1988 (Cth)* still apply.

¶8-020 Cash Transaction Reports and ASIC's Role

Under s 243D of the ASIC Act, a cash dealer is obliged to report the details of any suspect cash transactions under the *Financial Transaction Reports Act 1988 (Cth)*, to a range of bodies as listed in ss 243D(a) – (j) of the ASIC Act. This includes reporting to ASIC, under s 243D(a). A "cash dealer" can include, amongst others, a:

- financial institution or financial corporation,
- Australian Financial Services Licensee (AFSL) dealing in securities and derivatives,
- insurance company,
- Registrar or trustee,
- currency exchange business, issuing travellers cheques or money orders, or
- bookmaker or casino operator.

¶8-030 ASIC's Role in Anti-Money Laundering and Counter-Terrorism Financing

Section 243E of the ASIC Act states that s 123 of the *Anti-Money Laundering and Counter-Terrorism Financing Act 2006 (Cth)*, (which contains the offence of tipping off), does not prevent a party from disclosing information referred to in s 123 of that Act, to a specified body, including ASIC, s 243E(a) of the ASIC Act, or in accordance with certain provisions of the Corporations Act, ss 243E(d) – (i) of the ASIC Act.

¶8-040 Review of ASIC Decisions by the Administrative Appeals Tribunal

Under s 244 of the ASIC Act, the Administrative Appeals Tribunal can review decisions made by ASIC, including:

- a s 72 order in relation to securities of a body corporate
- a s 73 order in relation to financial products generally
- a s 75 order varying an order, or a decision to refuse to vary or revoke an order
- exemption decisions in relation to add-on insurance products
- decisions in relation to enforceable undertakings and the Financial Services and Credit Panel.

These decisions, made under specific provisions of the ASIC Act, "seize" the Administrative Appeals Tribunal with jurisdiction. When reviewing a decision of ASIC, the Administrative Appeals Tribunal stands in place of ASIC and "is empowered to exercise all of the relevant powers and discretions of ASIC for the purpose of reviewing the decision under review and hears the matter *de novo* in the light of the evidence and material placed before it": *ASIC v Donald* (2002) 20 ACLC 1. Hence, the power exercised by the Administrative Appeals Tribunal, standing in the shoes of ASIC, must be for the purpose of reviewing ASIC's decision.

If ASIC makes a decision to which s 244 of the ASIC Act applies, ASIC must then take reasonable steps to provide notice to parties whose interests are affected, including their rights to have the decision reviewed by the Administrative Appeals Tribunal, s 244A(2) of the ASIC Act. However, ASIC is not obliged to notify such parties if notification is not warranted due to cost or the way in which a party's interests are impacted, s 244A(3) of the ASIC

Act. Additionally, a failure by ASIC to advise an affected party does not necessarily invalidate ASIC's decision, s 244A(4) of the ASIC Act.

Section 1317B of the Corporations Act, also provides the Administrative Appeals Tribunal with jurisdiction to review decisions, including ASIC decisions made under the Corporations Act.

ASIC Regulatory Guide RG-57 – *Notification of rights of review* – sets out the obligations on ASIC to notify parties, affected by a decision of ASIC, including the fact that they have a right of appeal to the Administrative Appeals Tribunal.

¶8-050 Validity of Actions of ASIC Appointees

Under s 245 of the ASIC Act, the actions of a party (X) who has been appointed to an office under the ASIC Act remains valid even if X was not validly appointed (due to a defect or irregularity in appointment) or their appointment has ceased.

¶8-060 ASIC Liability for Damages

Section 246 of the ASIC Act provides an extensive list of parties who cannot be held liable for damages for an act or omission done, in good faith, in the performance of any function or power conferred under the ASIC Act, the Corporations Act or a prescribed law of the Commonwealth, a State or Territory. ASIC is included in this list of exempted parties, pursuant to ss 246(1)(a) and (c) of the ASIC Act.

In *Re Buddies Investments Pty Ltd* (1997) 15 ACLC 294, ASIC erroneously recorded the address of a company's registered office. The company was ultimately wound up because it failed to receive (and hence respond to) statutory demands. Although ASIC was protected from liability (under the equivalent of section 246 of the ASIC Act), it was ordered to pay the costs of all parties to the application to set aside the liquidator's appointment.

Whilst ASIC has no liability for damages under s 246 of the ASIC Act, the section does not go so far as to say that ASIC is not responsible for covering the costs of its investigation: *ASIC v Krecichwost* (2008) 26 ACLC 908.

¶8-070 Signatures and Seals

Sections 247 and 248 of the ASIC Act deal with signatures and company seals. ASIC can direct that there be duplicate common seals, s 247(1) of the ASIC Act. Under s 247(2) of the ASIC Act, affixing a duplicate seal to a document is deemed to be the same as affixing the common seal.

Under s 248(1) of the ASIC Act, a court must take judicial notice of a common seal affixed to a document and must assume that it was duly affixed, unless the contrary is proved. A court must also take judicial notice of the official signature of the ASIC Chairperson or ASIC Deputy Chairperson if their signature appears on an official document. For the purposes of s 248 of the ASIC Act, the terms "court" and "tribunal" are used interchangeably, ss 248(3)(a) and (b) of the ASIC Act.

Chapter 9

TRANSITIONAL PROVISIONS OF THE ASIC ACT

As discussed in Chapter 1, and specifically at ¶1-010, the 2001 ASIC Act essentially re-enacted the 1989 ASIC Act, as a Commonwealth Act capable of national operation. Hence, because of this re-enactment, the existing ASIC Act contains several transitional provisions for operational, functional and historical purposes.

Sections 253 – 285 of the ASIC Act, contain the transitional provisions. This chapter discusses these transitional provisions in assisting ASIC in the ongoing performance of its various roles.

¶9-000 Objectives of the Transitional Provisions

Section 253 of the ASIC Act defines the objective of the transitional provisions in providing for a smooth transition from the previous applied laws regime (in each State and Territory) to a national regulation. The objective is to ensure that parties are put in the position they would have been in under the old ASIC law.

It should be noted that the current ASIC Act contains provisions which correspond to most of the provisions of the old ASIC legislation.

¶9-010 Old ASIC Legislation

Section 254 of the ASIC Act defines "Old ASIC legislation" to include the relevant ASIC Act, laws and regulations, instruments made under them and other applicable State legislation.

¶9-020 Deemed Events

Under s 256 of the ASIC Act, if a State or Territory law deemed an event to have happened, or to have had a particular effect under the old ASIC legislation, then that continues to be the case under the new ASIC Act.

¶9-030 Penalty Units

Section 258 of the ASIC Act provides that a penalty unit for offences prosecuted for conduct under the old ASIC legislation, is to remain at $100, despite any contrary statement under s 4AA of the Crimes Act.

¶9-040 Cessation of State Referral

Under s 259 of the ASIC Act, if a State ceases to be a referring State, that does not undo the effects which the transitional provisions have already had in matters in that State.

¶9-050 Corporate Entities

Section 261 of the ASIC Act, states that a corporate body established under the old ASIC legislation continues to exist as if it had been established under the new Act. This includes ASIC.

¶9-060 Old ASIC Regulations

Section 264 of the ASIC Act confirms that the old ASIC regulations continue to have effect to the extent that they correspond to provisions of the present ASIC Act and were in force immediately prior to the new Act commencing.

¶9-070 Non-Federal ASIC Proceedings

Under s 267 of the ASIC Act, if a proceeding is not a federal ASIC proceeding or an enforcement, appeal or review proceeding relating to a court order, an equivalent new proceeding is taken to be on foot in the same court exercising federal jurisdiction

¶9-080 Federal ASIC Proceedings

Section 268 of the ASIC Act states that federal ASIC proceedings continue under this provision, s 268(3) of the ASIC Act, subject to the court's power to make contrary orders under s 268(4) of the ASIC Act.

¶9-090 Court Orders

Section 268A of the ASIC Act, enables court orders made under the old ASIC legislation to be enforced, or to be appealed or reviewed, under the existing ASIC Act.

¶9-100 Preservation of Decisions and Orders

Section 268B of the ASIC Act preserves the effect of decisions and orders made under the old ASIC legislation. Section 269 of the ASIC Act preserves the effect of steps taken in proceedings under the old ASIC legislation.

¶9-110 Rights and Liabilities

Sections 271 and 272 of the ASIC Act create rights and liabilities in non-Federal proceedings.

¶9-120 Relationship between the Transitional Provisions

Under ss 273 and 274 of the ASIC Act, the transitional provisions operate subject to, and in support of, the other transitional provisions and regulations. Hence, these provisions can overlap or interact with the other transitional provisions and are not intended to be mutually exclusive.

¶9-130 Exclusions from the Transitional Provisions

Section 273 of the ASIC Act confirms that the general transitional provisions under Pt 16, Div 6 of the ASIC Act, do not apply to court orders, appeals or proceedings made before the new ASIC Act commenced.

¶9-140 Preservation of Actions

Under s 275 of the ASIC Act, actions done under, or for the purpose of, the old ASIC legislation which had an ongoing significance immediately before the new ASIC Act commenced, are taken to have been done under, or for the purpose of, the present ASIC Act. Such actions may include commencing a prosecution (s 49 of the ASIC Act), requiring the production of books for inspection (under Pt 3, Div 3 of the ASIC Act) or a notice served on a party to produce documents (s 33 of the ASIC Act).

¶9-150 Accrual of Rights and Liabilities

Sections 276 and 277 of the ASIC Act confirm that where rights and liabilities were acquired, accrued or incurred under the old ASIC legislation, an equivalent right or liability is acquired, accrued or incurred under the new legislation even if that relevant right or liability has since been repealed.

¶9-160 Preservation of Time Limits

Section 278 of the ASIC Act preserves, and honours, time limits which commenced running under the old ASIC legislation.

¶9-170 Preservation of Events, Circumstances and Things

Sections 279 and 280 of the ASIC Act preserve the significance of events occurring, circumstances which arose, or things under the old ASIC Act.

¶9-180 Carrying over References to Corresponding Law

Under ss 281 and 282 of the ASIC Act, any references in the present ASIC Act to another provision will be deemed, in relation to events under the old ASIC Act, to include a reference to the corresponding provision of the old ASIC Act. Section 283 of the ASIC Act contains similar provisions for ASIC instruments.

¶9-190 Old Transitional Provisions continue to have Effect

Under s 284 of the ASIC Act, old transitional provisions, in the old ASIC legislation, continue to have effect even though they are no longer included in the new ASIC Act.

¶9-200 Regulations to Support Transitional Matters

Section 285 of that ASIC Act states that regulations may be promulgated in order to assist ASIC in its role of dealing with any transitional matters.

Chapter 10

ASIC'S ROLE IN INTERNATIONAL ACTIVITIES

The majority of this publication focuses on ASIC's role as Australia's corporate regulator and how that role is regulated by the ASIC Act.

However, ASIC also has a significant role in working closely with a range of international organisations, foreign corporate regulators and law enforcement agencies to ensure corporate compliance at a global level.

As part of this role, ASIC makes and receives, international requests in relation to investigations, compliance and surveillance, policy research, delegations, licensing, due diligence and general referrals. ASIC's International Cooperation Requests team manages these operational requests on behalf of ASIC.

ASIC participates in a number of important international regulatory forums including the International Organisation of Securities Commissions (**IOSCO**). ASIC is also a signatory to several international cooperation agreements and bilateral Memoranda of Understanding (MoU), including the IOSCO MoU.

This chapter takes a deeper dive into ASIC's role at an international level.

For further information on ASIC's role in international activities refer to ASIC's website at https://www.asic.gov.au.

¶10-000 ASIC's Role in International Strategy, Forums and Technical Assistance

Financial markets, and the provision of financial services, are increasingly global in nature.

ASIC's role in developing international strategy

It is important for global regulators to engage with each other to ensure efficient, robust and sustainable financial markets, and to develop more effective international approaches to regulation and enforcement.

Through its international activities, ASIC seeks to:

- promote confident and informed financial investors,
- promote fair and efficient financial markets,
- engage with international policy forums,
- participate in international standard setting, and
- build relationships with foreign regulators.

Hence, ASIC's international team assists in co-ordinating and supporting ASIC's wider international activities.

ASIC's participation in key forums

ASIC participates in a number of important international policy forums. ASIC is a signatory to international cooperation agreements including the IOSCO Multilateral MoU and numerous bilateral memoranda of understanding.

International Organisation of Securities Commissions (IOSCO)

IOSCO is an international body. It brings together securities regulators from around the globe and is recognised as the global standard setter for the securities sector. IOSCO develops, implements and promotes adherence to internationally recognised standards for securities regulation. Part of ASIC's role is to actively participate in various IOSCO committees and task forces.

International Forum of Independent Audit Regulators (IFIAR)

IFIAR provides a forum for sharing knowledge of the audit market environment, as well as practical experiences in independent audit regulatory activity.

Corporate Registers Forum (CRF)

The CRF is an international not-for-profit (NFP) organisation for administrators of corporate and securities registers. ASIC has been on the executive of the CRF since its establishment in 2005.

International Association of Insolvency Regulators (IAIR)

IAIR is an international body which brings together the collective experiences and expertise of government insolvency regulators from jurisdictions around the world. IAIR members, such as ASIC, provide a unique perspective given the role which they play in insolvency systems.

Other forums

ASIC also contributes to whole-of-government initiatives in relation to the:

- Group of Twenty (**G20**),
- Organisation for Economic Cooperation and Development (**OECD**), and
- Asia-Pacific Economic Cooperation (**APEC**).

ASIC's role in providing technical assistance

ASIC has a role in providing training, and other technical assistance to other securities regulators in the Asia-Pacific region. For example, ASIC contributes speakers to the APEC Financial Regulators Training Initiative (FRTI). This initiative is designed to strengthen financial supervision and regulation in the Asia-Pacific region by enhancing the analytical and technical capacity of securities regulators and others. ASIC's role provides a sustainable and efficient training structure for staff of financial supervisory and regulatory agencies and exchanges.

ASIC's focus in providing technical assistance has been with the Indonesian Financial Services Authority. This role has involved providing workshops, seminars and incoming and outgoing secondments which are funded under the Australia-Indonesia Partnership for Reconstruction and Development's Government Partnership Fund. ASIC's aim is to strengthen the capacity of the Indonesian Financial Services Authority to:

- develop and implement global standards and best practices, and
- foster a culture of responsive and skills-based surveillance and risk-focused supervision, which can enable regulatory effort to be targeted where it can achieve the best results. This means making the best use of resources and drawing on the knowledge and expertise of staff of the Indonesian Financial Services Authority i.e. those with experience of best-practice regulation.

¶10-010 ASIC's Role in International Regulatory and Enforcement Cooperation

ASIC's role as a corporate regulator means it works closely with a range of global organisations, including foreign regulators and law enforcement agencies.

Many international organisations and foreign regulators make requests for assistance under international cooperation agreements such as the IOSCO Multilateral MoU and other bilateral Memoranda of Understanding. Where authorised, ASIC uses the *Mutual Assistance in Business Regulation Act 1992 (Cth)* to exercise compulsory powers to obtain documents, information or testimony on behalf of foreign regulators, when requested to do so.

To assist in determining the scale of ASIC's role in providing international assistance, in the 2011–12 financial year, ASIC dealt with a total of 429 requests from foreign regulators.

The following ASIC publications can assist in understanding ASIC's role at an international level:

- corporate plan,
- annual reports,
- quarterly updates,
- newsletters,
- media releases,
- gazette,
- digests,
- regulatory guides,
- information sheets,
- consultation papers, and
- corporate statistics.

ASIC's role under MoU concerning international cooperation

ASIC is a signatory to the IOSCO:

- Multilateral MoU
- Enhanced Multilateral MoU Concerning Consultation and Cooperation and the Exchange of Information, and
- Administrative Arrangement.

ASIC is also a signatory to international agreements with over 55 countries and entities, including Canada, the United States, United Kingdom, European Union, New Zealand, Singapore, Japan and China.

These agreements outline the relationship between the signing parties with regard to **mutual assistance** and the exchange of information for the purpose of enforcing and regulating the respective international laws and regulations of the signatories.

¶10-020 ASIC's Role in Overseas Regulators Public Warnings and Alerts

A certain number of global regulators publish public warnings and information on their websites about individuals, companies and other legal entities against whom legal or administrative action has been taken.

This assists in alerting other corporate regulators of potential offenders. This is particularly important in the event that an individual absconds to another jurisdiction or overseas, or a company under investigation attempts to set up operations in a foreign country.

Hence, the publication of such notices, ensures that all global regulators can work together in enforcing strict compliance with legislation and regulations governing corporate conduct. ASIC has an important role to play here as Australia's corporate watchdog.

Public warnings and alerts

Public warnings and alerts from global regulators can cover a broad range of topics, including alerts on:

- firms not authorised to provide investment services in the jurisdictions which issued the alert / warning
- information on enforcement actions by overseas regulators, including litigation, administrative proceedings, trading suspensions, stop orders, injunctions and accounting and auditing enforcement releases
- disciplinary history on registration and trading sanctions currently in effect as a result of administrative enforcement or statutory disqualification proceedings
- lists of disqualified directors (including a register of disqualified orders), disciplined persons and investor alerts
- recent and searchable historical details for entities and individuals
- information on fraud investigations and prosecutions involving both corporate entities and directors.

ASIC also maintains and publishes a list of global companies to avoid doing business with. This list is available to download from ASIC's Smart Money website. The companies on this list:

- have made unsolicited calls and emails about financial services and products, and/or
- do not hold a current AFSL or Australian credit licence from ASIC, which is required in order to practice as a financial service provider.

¶10-030 ASIC's Role in Global Licencing Due Diligence and Probity Information

As part of its role, ASIC may receive requests from an overseas financial services regulator for due diligence or probity information, as part of its licensing or registration process. ASIC supports this regulator-to-regulator practice as part of its role of monitoring and promoting market integrity and consumer protection in relation to Australia's financial system.

Overseas financial services regulator checks

ASIC provides a wealth of information to overseas financial services regulators which can assist them with their licensing or registration process. This includes information contained in ASIC's public registers, including whether a company or an individual holds an AFSL or is a banned and/or disqualified person.

Overseas regulators can also find useful information by searching:

- ASIC media releases,
- The Enforceable Undertakings Register, and
- Summary prosecutions of companies and directors

Refer to ¶7-110 of this publication for more detailed information on enforceable undertakings.

It is important to note that ASIC does not register or licence individual participants in the financial services industry unless that individual is carrying on a financial services business as a sole trader. Individuals who are, or have been, "authorised representatives" of financial services licensees are publicly listed on the Australian Financial Services (AFS) Authorised Representatives Register.

Information which ASIC can and cannot provide to an overseas financial services regulator

If an overseas financial services regulator fails to find the required information on ASIC's public registers or website, they may make a probity request for confidential information. ASIC will release confidential information in accordance with their statutory obligations which are outlined in Regulatory Guide 103 (RG-103) – *Confidentiality and release of information*.

There are certain categories of non-public information which, as a general rule, AISC will not release in response to a probity check response. These categories include:

- complaints made to AISC where ASIC has assessed the complaint and determined that no regulatory action is required,
- minor technical matters, such as a single instance of failure to lodge an annual report within the stipulated timeframe,
- concluded surveillances which failed to raise any material concerns, or which resulted in no further action being taken by ASIC, and

- highly confidential and/or commercially or market-sensitive information; for example, prior knowledge of a particular takeover bid.

ASIC will generally not conduct searches for confidential or non-public information beyond a period of 5 years.

ASIC may contact companies or individual parties when considering whether to release confidential information but will not disclose any regulator-to-regulator correspondence to those companies or parties. Nor will ASIC provide letters of support to companies or individual parties in relation to their personal dealings with foreign regulators.

ASIC will ordinarily respond to a standard probity request within 28 days of receipt of all the required information. However, more complex matters may require additional time.

When will ASIC respond to a probity check request?

ASIC will apply certain thresholds to determine whether it is appropriate to respond to a probity check request. These thresholds are the:

- jurisdictional nexus of the nature of the request with Australia. ASIC generally expects that an overseas regulator, who is conducting a probity check request about an individual or entity, will demonstrate why this individual or entity has a connection with Australia; for example, the individual has worked in the Australian financial services industry.
- reason for the probity request; for example, the information is required in order to comply with statutory obligations or to assist with assessing a licence application. An overseas regulator may also seek ASIC's assistance if it has a suspicion that an applicant has failed to disclose relevant information in its application for a licence.

In addition, AISC also requires probity requests to include details concerning the company, legal entity or individual, such as an individual's name and date of birth, in order to assist ASIC in conducting the relevant searches of their confidential databases.

AISC Information Sheet 92 (INFO 92) – *Probity request procedures for overseas regulators* – provides further information on the processes which overseas regulators must go through in order to validly request a probity check from ASIC. This Information Sheet covers the:

- circumstances in which a probity check is possible,
- information which ASIC will and will not provide in a probity check, and
- information publicly available on ASIC's website.

¶10-040 ASIC's Role in Handling Requests for Visits by Foreign Delegations

ASIC may be requested to host a foreign delegation.

ASIC typically only accepts delegations from international organisations, foreign regulators and law enforcement agencies. However, ASIC may, under exceptional circumstances, accept requests from non-government or non-regulatory agencies.

Requests for visits to ASIC require detailed topics for discussion and/or questions. ASIC will generally not provide an overview of ASIC's functions, the Australian regulatory system or meet with foreign delegations seeking operational information.

A request to ASIC must be accompanied by detailed information including:

- full contact details,
- the purpose of the proposed visit,
- specific topics for discussion,
- whether the visit is government-funded or privately sponsored,
- a list of any other organisations to be visited within Australia, and
- particulars (including dates) of any other recent visits to ASIC by members of the organisation proposing the visit.

Such detailed information must be provided to ASIC at least 4 weeks prior to the proposed visit, in order to afford ASIC sufficient time to prepare.

TABLE OF CASES

Paragraph

A

Paragraph

Paragraph

Paragraph

TABLE OF LEGISLATION

COMMONWEALTH

Acts Interpretation Act 1901

Administrative Decisions (Judicial Review) Act 1977

Anti-Money Laundering and Counter-Terrorism Financing Act 2006

ASIC Supervisory Cost Recovery Levy Regulations 2017

Australian Consumer Law

Australian Prudential Regulation Authority Act 1998

Australian Securities and Investments Commission Act 2001

Australian Securities and Investments Commission (ASIC) Regulation

Australian Securities Commission Act 1989

Bankruptcy Act 1966

Business Names Registration Act 2011

Competition and Consumer Act 2010

Constitution

Corporations Act 2001

Corporations Legislation Amendment (Audit Enhancement) Act 2012

Crimes Act 1914

Director of Public Prosecutions Act 1983

Evidence Act 1995

Federal Court of Australia Act 1976

Financial Sector Reform (Amendments and Transitional Provisions) Act (No 1) 1999

Financial Sector Reform (Hayne Royal Commission Response - Better Advice) Act 2021

Financial Sector Reform (Hayne Royal Commission Response) Act 2020

Financial Transaction Reports Act 1988

Insurance Act 1973

Insurance Contracts Act 1984

Judiciary Act 1903

Legislation Act 2003

Life Insurance Act 1995

Mutual Assistance in Business Regulation Act 1992

National Consumer Credit Protection Act 2009

National Consumer Credit Protection (Transitional and Consequential Provisions) Act 2009

National Credit Code

Privacy Act 1988

Public Governance, Performance and Accountability Act 2013

Superannuation Industry (Supervision) Act 1993

Tax Agent Services Act 2009

Telecommunications (Interception and Access) Act 1979

Treasury Laws Amendment (Australian Consumer Law Review) Act 2018

Treasury Laws Amendment (Enhancing ASIC's Capabilities) Act 2018

Treasury Laws Amendment (Strengthening Corporate and Financial Sector Penalties) Act 2019

INDEX

Made in the USA
Las Vegas, NV
12 April 2026

45209971R00096